Globalization and the Perceptions of American Workers

Globalization and the Perceptions of American Workers

**Kenneth F. Scheve and
Matthew J. Slaughter**

Institute for International Economics
Washington, DC
March 2001

Kenneth F. Scheve is assistant professor of political science at Yale University and a resident fellow at the university's Institution for Social and Policy Studies. He has recently been a visiting researcher at the Bank of England and the Center for Basic Research in the Social Sciences at Harvard University.

Matthew J. Slaughter, visiting fellow, is assistant professor of economics at Dartmouth College, a faculty research fellow of the National Bureau of Economic Research, and a term member of the Council on Foreign Relations. He has been a visiting scholar at the International Monetary Fund and the Federal Reserve Bank of Minneapolis, and a consultant to the World Bank, the Department of Labor, and the Emergency Committee for American Trade.

INSTITUTE FOR INTERNATIONAL ECONOMICS
11 Dupont Circle, NW
Washington, DC 20036-1207
(202) 328-9000 FAX: (202) 328-5432
http://www.iie.com

C. Fred Bergsten, *Director*
Brigitte Coulton, *Director of Publications and Web Development*
Brett Kitchen, *Director of Marketing*

Typesetting and printing by Automated Graphic Systems

Printed in the United States of America
03 02 01 5 4 3 2 1

Library of Congress Cataloging-in-Publication Data

Slaughter, Matthew J. (Matthew Jon)
   Globalization and the perceptions of American Workers / Kenneth F. Scheve, Matthew J. Slaughter.
      p. cm.
   Includes bibliographical references and index.
   1. Foreign trade and employment—United States. 2. Globalization. 3. Investments, Foreign, and employment—United States.

HD5710.75.U6 S53 2000
331.1'0973—dc21   00-063286

ISBN 0-88132-295-4

Contents

Figures

Tables

Preface

The Institute has published a number of studies that address various aspects of the globalization issue, including *Fighting the Wrong Enemy: Antiglobal Activists and Multinational Enterprises* (2000) by Edward M. Graham; *The WTO after Seattle* (2000) edited by Jeffrey J. Schott; *Is the US Trade Deficit Sustainable?* (1999) by Catherine L. Mann; and *Has Globalization Gone Too Far?* (1997) by Dani Rodrik. This book is the first in the Institute's new Globalization Balance Sheet series, a multiyear family of analyses undertaken to evaluate the impact of international economic integration on the United States. The series will include a wide-ranging set of studies to measure the tangible gains and losses from globalization, enabling us both to discern how much reality underlies the claims of opponents of the phenomenon and to determine how to minimize the real losses that can result from the process.

There is widespread agreement among policymakers, economists, and the business community that a globalization backlash is underway in many countries. In the United States, those rejecting further globalization have gained considerable ground. New trade negotiating authority has been stalled since 1994. Serious opposition was witnessed during the 1999 WTO ministerial conference in Seattle and the 2000 IMF/World Bank meetings in Washington. The congressional vote on permanent normal trade relations for China in 2000, which should have been routine, was highly contentious and closely contested.

A common characterization of this backlash is that globalization—liberalization of trade, increased foreign investment, and rising immigration—is opposed by relatively small interest groups with agendas that are not directly related to the economics of the phenomenon. High-profile media coverage of the Seattle and Washington demonstrations suggests that such small groups stalled the talks.

This book documents evidence to the contrary. Through an analysis of public opinion polls and other empirical material, authors Kenneth F. Scheve and Matthew J. Slaughter show that the backlash resonates with widespread skepticism among US citizens and that the public—like the Congress—is evenly split over globalization. These public perceptions seem to be closely connected to the pressures that globalization may be imparting on US workers. The central message in the book is that the education and skill levels of individual Americans largely determine their attitudes toward globalization, and that popular support for further liberalization is likely to be conditioned on effective governmental assistance to help workers adjust to its adverse effects.

The authors base their conclusions on three key findings. First, a wide range of public opinion surveys indicates that US citizens recognize both the costs and benefits of global economic integration but that they tend to weigh the costs more than the benefits and support further liberalization only if the losers in the process are assisted in meeting their transition requirements. Second, these policy preferences differ markedly across labor skill and education levels. Less-skilled workers—measured by educational attainment or wages earned—are much more likely to oppose freer trade and immigration than their more-skilled counterparts. Third, these differences in skill and education levels may reflect very different wage growth across skill groups in the US labor market since the early 1970s. Less-skilled US workers—a group that still constitutes the majority of the US labor force—have experienced close to zero or even negative real-wage growth, despite renewed progress in recent years, and have also seen sharp declines in their wages relative to more-skilled workers.

This book addresses the backlash only in the United States although the phenomenon is apparent in other countries as well. There are several reasons for this focus: the United States is by far the largest national economy and thus plays a critical role in global economic affairs; it has traditionally been a leader in the globalization policymaking process and the domestic political stalemate has severely hampered its ability to lead, or even to participate effectively, in recent years; and it has a vast bank of data that permits a reasonably accurate analysis of the backlash. Moreover, the backlash in the United States has profound global effects and this study thus carries implications far beyond the United States itself. In addition, we hope that the methodologies developed for the several components of our Globalization Balance Sheet series will subsequently be applied to other countries, both developed and developing, and that a number of comparable national analyses will be generated over the next few years.

The Institute for International Economics is a private nonprofit institution for the study and discussion of international economic policy. Its purpose is to analyze important issues in that area and develop and communicate practical new approaches for dealing with them. The Institute is completely nonpartisan.

The Institute is funded largely by philanthropic foundations. Major institutional grants are now being received from the William M. Keck, Jr. Foundation and the Starr Foundation. A number of other foundations and private corporations contribute to the highly diversified financial resources of the Institute. Partial funding for the Institute's Globalization Balance Sheet series is being provided by the Toyota Motor Corporation, in light of the great interest in these issues in both the United States and Japan. The Andrew W. Mellon Foundation is also supporting these studies. About 26 percent of the Institute's resources in our latest fiscal year were provided by contributors outside the United States, including about 11 percent from Japan.

The Board of Directors bears overall responsibility for the Institute and gives general guidance and approval to its research program—including the identification of topics that are likely to become important over the medium run (one to three years), and which should be addressed by the Institute. The Director, working closely with the staff and outside Advisory Committee, is responsible for the development of particular projects and makes the final decision to publish an individual study.

The Institute hopes that its studies and other activities will contribute to building a stronger foundation for international economic policy around the world. We invite readers of these publications to let us know how they think we can best accomplish this objective.

C. Fred Bergsten
Director
February 2001

Acknowledgments

This study has benefited significantly from the comments and suggestions of a number of scholars. We especially thank John Aldrich, Robert Baldwin, Ted Brader, Richard Cooper, John Freeman, Geoff Garrett, Doug Irwin, Thomas Paley, and David Richardson who read a preliminary draft of the manuscript and provided written comments. We also thank Fred Bergsten, Kim Elliot, Howard Lewis, Theodore Moran, Howard Rosen, and related researchers on the Globalization Balance Sheet project at the Institute for International Economics for their suggestions and Brigitte Coulton, Madona Devasahayam, and Marla Banov for their superb work in preparing the book for publication.

We also thank Jim Alt, Patty Anderson, Danny Blanchflower, Irene Bloemraad, George Borjas, Lawrence Broz, Gary Freeman, Jeffry Frieden, Jim Harrigan, James Honaker, Torben Iversen, Alan Kessler, Gary King, Ed Leamer, Jim Levinsohn, Jonathan Nagler, Sharyn O'Halloran, Alejandro Poiré, Ron Rogowski, Charles Stewart, and Michael Tomz for their helpful comments.

We acknowledge the financial support of the Bank of England, the Center for Basic Research in the Social Sciences at Harvard University, the Institution for Social and Policy Studies at Yale University, the National Bureau of Economic Research, the National Science Foundation, the Russell Sage Foundation, the Rockefeller Center for Public Policy at Dartmouth College, and the Weatherhead Center for International Affairs.

Part of this study draws on our joint research in Scheve and Slaughter (2001a, 2001b), published in the *Journal of International Economics* and the *Review of Economics and Statistics*. We thank Elsevier Science and MIT Press for permission to present some of that research here.

Finally, for generous assistance in gathering data we thank Clark Bensen, George Borjas, Karolyn Bowman, John Cocklin, Gary Engelhardt, Michael Ferrantino, Annamaria Lusardi, and Jonathan Skinner.

1

Introduction

Today in the United States—and many other countries as well—there appears to be significant opposition to policies aimed at further liberalization of international trade, immigration, and foreign direct investment (FDI). A large number of political events in recent years suggest a marked turn away from liberalization, and many prominent observers have raised alarms about this "globalization backlash."

For example, in August 2000, Federal Reserve Chairman Alan Greenspan acknowledged that liberalization efforts had stalled and outbreaks of protectionism were a distinct possibility: "Despite extraordinary prosperity, the ability to move forward on various trade initiatives has clearly come to a remarkable stall . . . there remains considerable unease among some segments [of society] about the way markets distribute wealth and about the effects of raw competition on society. . . . It is quite imaginable that support for market-oriented resource allocation will wane and the latent forces of protectionism and state intervention will begin to reassert themselves in many countries, including the United States" (*New York Times*, 26 August 2000).

What exactly is meant by globalization? For our analysis, we define globalization as the increased integration of product and factor markets across countries via trade, immigration, and FDI—that is, via cross-border flows of goods and services, of people, and of capital linked with multinational firms. Our analysis excludes cross-border flows of financial capital; these flows have surely been important in recent years (e.g., exchange rate crises in Europe in 1992 and 1993 and worldwide between 1997 and 1999), but they entail many macroeconomic issues beyond the scope of our microeconomic analysis of individuals.

Figure 1.1   Globalization in terms of US imports and exports as a share of GDP

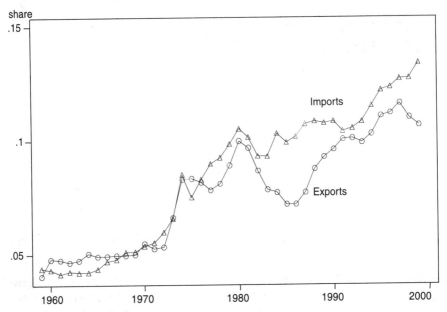

Source: Bureau of Economic Analysis, US Census Bureau. http://www.bea.doc.gov.

Note that we delineate globalization as an economic phenomenon. We acknowledge that a broader definition includes noneconomic elements such as culture and the environment (see Keohane and Nye 2000 for a discussion of globalization's many components). Our economic perspective highlights the role of labor-market interests and pressures in shaping perceptions of and preferences about globalization, a role that has been relatively underanalyzed. This is not to diminish the importance of noneconomic aspects of globalization, nor to deny the possibility of issue linkages between economic and noneconomic concerns. Indeed, in our empirical analysis we explicitly address how other, noneconomic issues may be related to individual preferences about economic globalization.

Figures 1.1, 1.2, and 1.3 offer three images of globalization at work on the US economy in recent decades. Figure 1.1 plots US exports and imports, each as a share of US gross domestic product (GDP). Figure 1.2 plots the share of the total US population that is foreign born, and figure 1.3 plots the market value of total US inward and outward FDI stocks, each as a share of GDP. All three figures show rising flows of goods and services, people, and multinational capital across US borders in recent decades.[1]

---

1. Note that figures 1.1 through 1.3 all show quantity evidence of market integration across borders. For many issues, economists think that price evidence is at least as important, if not more so.

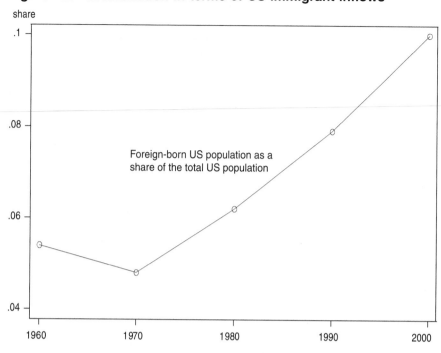

Figure 1.2   Globalization in terms of US immigrant inflows

share

Foreign-born US population as a
share of the total US population

Note: Data for the year 2000 are estimated.

Source: Borjas et al. (1997, table 1).

What drives this process of globalization? In the models of economists, important forces include differences across countries in consumer tastes, production technologies, and factor supplies. But another key force in the process may be declining barriers, both natural and political, to cross-border flows. In recent decades natural trade barriers have declined thanks to advances in communications, information, and shipping technologies (e.g., fax machines, the Internet, and wide-body jets). What role have political barriers played? Some kinds of political trade barriers have fallen around the world in recent decades—for example, average tariffs, thanks largely to the General Agreement on Tariffs and Trade and other treaties.

Many other kinds of political trade barriers, however, have not been falling but instead have been holding steady or even rising. For example, antidumping filings have increased sharply in recent decades in the United States and many other countries (Prusa 1999). It is precisely this kind of political resistance to further policy liberalization that is often cited as evidence of a rising globalization backlash.

To make things concrete, here is a summary of several recent US events commonly cited as examples of the backlash. These events surely involved

Figure 1.3 Globalization in terms of US inward and outward FDI stock as a share of GDP

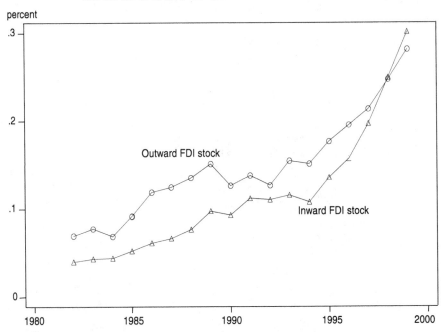

Source: Scholl (2000, table 2).

issues beyond globalization, but opposition to globalization seems to have played a prominent role in all of them.

- *Inability to renew "fast-track" negotiating authority.* The Trade Act of 1974 granted the president the ability to negotiate trade agreements with carefully delineated congressional oversight. Once the president reached an agreement in principle, Congress had to vote yea or nay on the agreement in a fixed period of time without the option of attaching amendments. Congress renewed fast track in 1979, 1988, 1991, and 1993. But in 1997, after pushing for a bill renewing fast-track authority, President Clinton asked House Speaker Newt Gingrich to kill House consideration of the bill after the White House concluded it did not have enough votes for passage. In 1998 fast-track renewal was again considered in the House; this time it came to a vote, but it was defeated 243 to 180, with over 80 percent of the president's own party voting against renewal.

- *Public protests over the 1999 WTO ministerial meetings in Seattle and over the 2000 IMF/World Bank annual meetings in Washington.* At both these meetings, tens of thousands of protesters representing a wide range of interest groups severely disrupted official proceedings (especially in Seattle), all with the attention of worldwide media coverage. At least 30,000 members of the American Federation of Labor and Congress of Industrial Organizations (AFL-CIO) marched in various protest rallies aimed against freer trade. Trade was the central issue in Seattle; at the Washington IMF/Bank meetings, it was a major issue along with international finance issues such as external-debt relief for highly indebted countries and conditionality of IMF/Bank loans. Many commentators have credited the size and severity of the Seattle protests with contributing to the failure of the WTO delegates to initiate a new round of negotiations. Positions taken by the US delegation—arguing for labor standards to enter the WTO agenda, refusing to accelerate Multifiber Arrangement phase-outs, and refusing to countenance restrictions on US antidumping filings—were widely criticized as protectionist obstacles.

- *China-US trade agreement.* The most volatile US trade issue in 2000 was the vote in the House of Representatives on whether to grant permanent normal trade relations (PNTR) status to China. This plan passed more easily in the Senate, but the House vote was widely regarded as very close in the preceding months. The US labor movement waged a massive opposition campaign, "its biggest lobbying campaign ever on trade matters," according to a *New York Times* front-page story (14 May 2000). On 12 April, thousands of AFL-CIO members rallied on Capitol Hill and lobbied dozens of House members against the bill.

  The bill finally passed in the House on 24 May by a 237-197 vote, but with many free trade supporters concerned about the intensity of opposition. For example, Albert R. Hunt worried in the *Wall Street Journal* that the "vote on free trade with China was a warning shot for free traders, the business community, and labor groups. . . . More remarkable than the passage, however, was how tough it was to approve a measure so demonstrably beneficial. Americans are currently enjoying the best economy ever. If it's a struggle to pass free-trade bills in this environment, what would it be like in less bullish times?" (*Wall Street Journal*, 25 May 2000, A27).

- *The African Growth and Opportunity Act.* This bill will liberalize trade with dozens of small, vulnerable countries in Africa; in particular, it proposes eliminating a 17 percent ad valorem tariff on US imports of African clothing. The bill passed through Congress in May 2000, after having been stalled for almost five years in the face of sharp opposition widely regarded as led by the major US textile union, the Union of Needleworkers, Industrial, and Textile Trades Employees (UNITE), and by the American Textile Manufacturers Institute.

  This opposition was widely thought to be driven by groups opposed to freer trade. Thomas L. Friedman argued in the *New York Times* that the opposition stemmed from "sheer knee-jerk protectionism—even though the bill has tough measures to protect against any surge in imports from Africa, and restricts free-trade status to African countries moving toward democracy, economic reform, and real worker protection" (*New York Times*, 7 March 2000). And the actual liberalization is modest, with tariff reductions accompanied by strict quotas: African duty-free clothing imports cannot exceed 1.5 percent of all US textile imports in the first year of the law, with the cap rising to only 3.5 percent after eight years.

■ *Debate surrounding the 1993 congressional vote on the North American Free Trade Agreement (NAFTA).* The summer and fall of 1993 saw intense national debate over whether the United States should extend the Canadian-US free trade agreement to include Mexico. Destler (1995, 217) called these discussions "the most prominent and contentious domestic debate on trade since the Smoot-Hawley Tariff Act of 1930." NAFTA opposition was led by Ross Perot, who as an independent candidate received 19.1 percent of the popular vote in the 1992 presidential election. The debate reached a rhetorical peak on 9 November with a nationally televised prime-time face-off between Perot and Vice President Al Gore on *Larry King Live,* just days before the House vote. Gore was widely perceived as the winner of this debate; his performance, plus intense White House lobbying, helped the House pass the NAFTA on 17 November by a vote of 234 to 200.

■ *Death of the Multilateral Agreement on Investment.* In December 1998, the Organization for Economic Cooperation and Development halted its efforts to ratify among its members a new FDI treaty aimed at ensuring that host governments treat domestic and foreign-owned firms equally. It is widely believed that a significant force behind the collapse of this agreement was intense lobbying efforts of nongovernmental organizations, whose tactics included posting on the Internet a smuggled draft of the treaty. After three years, negotiations halted in April 1998 for additional discussion among relevant parties. Negotiations never fully resumed, however, and in December that year, efforts ceased. (See Graham 2000 for details.)

■ *New immigration restrictions.* Border enforcement policies have toughened considerably in recent years. In 1994, California voters approved Proposition 187, which denied public services such as public education and health care to illegal immigrants. Since 1997, legislation has barred the use of federal money to cover Medicaid costs for poor legal immigrants during their first five years of residence.

Taken together, these events suggest that a globalization backlash is under way in the United States. But what forces underlie this backlash?

It has commonly been characterized as reflecting the interests of a collection of relatively small groups whose diverse agendas have very little connection, if any, with the economic consequences of policy liberalization. This view has been prominent in the media coverage of high-profile backlash episodes such as the protests in Seattle and Washington.

For example, Rich Miller (*Business Week*, 24 April 2000, 46-47) calls the protesters "a curious bunch. . . . There are intellectuals who believe the IMF bungled the Asian crisis. And there's an amorphous amalgam of Gen Y college students and aging baby boomers united by their abhorrence of big business. Organizers are using the Internet and the promise of plenty of street theater, music, and giant allegorical puppets to entice the young to turn out." Writing about Seattle, Friedman observed, "The environmentalists and the unions—and the stone-throwing anarchists who joined them—are not organic allies, with a shared agenda. (God save any turtle that gets in the way of the dockworkers unloading a boat. You wouldn't want to be that turtle.)" (*New York Times*, 1 February 2000) And *The Economist* declared the protesters to be devoid of clear thought: "This week's grotesque pantomime in Seattle suggests that this horrible prospect [of stalled WTO progress] needs to be thought about. To say this is not to support the preposterous non-arguments with which the WTO has been assailed these past few days . . . all these claims are either meaningless or demonstrably false" (4 December 1999).

This consensus view of the protesters presents an incomplete picture of the globalization backlash, however, because it does not take into account the views of the broader population. What, if anything, do people think about the liberalization of trade, immigration, and FDI? To what extent do these backlash events resonate with the broader public? Are policy attitudes commonly held, or do they divide along particular lines? Are such cleavages related to the actual economic impacts of globalization?

To fully understand the globalization backlash, it is essential to investigate the policy attitudes of US citizens. In this book we analyze the *perceptions* and policy *preferences* of US citizens and workers toward globalization and then compare these perceptions and preferences to the labor-market *pressures* that globalization may be imparting to the US economy.[2] We generate an account of the globalization backlash that differs sharply from the consensus described above. We argue that the backlash reflects

---

2. This analysis draws on our work in Scheve and Slaughter (2001a, b). It is related to a large body of research linking the politics of globalization to mass politics, including Aldrich et al. (1999a, b), Anderson and Kaltenthaler (1996), Busch and Reinhardt (2000), Citrin et al. (1997), Eichenberg and Dalton (1993), Espenshade and Hempstead (1996), Frieden (1991), Friedman (2000), Gabel (1998a, b), Garrett (1998), Greider (1997), Hiscox (1997), Irwin (1994; 1996), Kapstein (1999), Kessler (1998), Midford (1993), PIPA (2000), Rodrik (1997), Rogowski (1987; 1989), Timmer and Williamson (1998), Verdier (1994), and Wallach and Sforza (1999).

widespread skepticism among US citizens about globalization and that these perceptions seem to be closely connected to the labor-market pressures globalization may be imparting to US workers.

Our account focuses on just one country, the United States. The most important reason is that in recent decades the United States has been at the forefront of shaping policy discussions surrounding globalization and a substantial backlash against liberalization in the United States would be felt around the world. The United States, however, is by no means unique; many other countries have liberalized international exchange or experienced backlash against such policies, but we think the US experience is particularly informative.[3]

The remainder of this introductory chapter summarizes our findings. Our analysis starts with a detailed look at the perceptions and policy preferences of US citizens, as documented in public opinion surveys. We start here because policy *actions*—such as the actions against globalization listed above—are the outcome of the interaction between policy preferences, collective-action problems, and political institutions.[4] Policy preferences, collective-action problems, and institutions together determine policy actions, so the link between preferences and actions is not unambiguous. The globalization backlash could be consistent with many different policy preferences. For example, globalization opponents may be only a small minority of the US population, concentrated in particular groups (socioeconomic, or geographic, or industrial) with a narrow set of concerns, such that the backlash does not reflect majority opinions. Alternatively, globalization opponents may be a large majority of the US population, with broadly shared concerns. To make sense of the backlash, it is essential to know what is going on with public preferences. We acknowledge that understanding policy preferences alone is not sufficient for completely understanding policy actions. Our analysis will not go beyond preferences to consider how preferences are aggregated via institutions into particular globalization policies. Thus, we will not offer to explain Seattle, the China PNTR vote, and the like, but rather the public preferences helping to shape these actions.[5]

---

3. Additional research exploring both similarities and differences among countries in public opinion about globalization will help put our analysis in perspective. See Scheve (2000) for one analysis explaining systematic differences between countries in public opinion about one particular form of globalization—regional economic integration.

4. By collective-action problems, we refer to the common situation in which individuals or firms would be better off if they contributed to a common effort (e.g., protesting or lobbying for policy changes), but have no incentive to do so individually or as a single firm.

5. Rodrik (1995) makes this distinction between preferences and actions when arguing that a complete political economy model of trade policy "must contain a description of how these individual preferences are aggregated and channeled, through pressure groups, political parties, or grass-roots movements, into 'political demands' for a particular policy." Studies relating preferences with actions include Destler (1995) and Baldwin and Magee

One key finding is that the backlash does reflect significant opposition among US citizens toward globalization. A wide range of public opinion surveys report that a plurality or a majority of US citizens oppose policies to further liberalize trade, immigration, and FDI. On some issues the public is evenly split, but even this divide reflects substantial skepticism about globalization. These perceptions do not simply reflect ignorance about the economic benefits of liberalization. On the contrary, the majority of those surveyed acknowledge gains from international transactions, such as greater product variety, lower import prices, and increased product-market competition for producers. But at the same time, the majority also have concerns about these transactions, in particular their adverse labor-market impacts. On balance, more people seem to weigh these costs as more important than the benefits, such that across a wide range of survey questions they respond with preferences for policies aimed at less, not more, liberalization of trade, immigration, and FDI. This connection between individual preferences and the labor-market effects of liberalization is further confirmed by evidence that opinions become more favorable toward liberalization when it is explicitly linked to adjustment assistance for workers.

A second key finding is that preferences about trade and immigration policy align strongly with labor-market skills.[6] Less-skilled individuals, measured by educational attainment or wages earned, are much more likely to oppose freer trade and immigration than their more-skilled counterparts. For example, our analysis suggests that the probability that an American supports trade protection falls by about 30 percentage points when that American increases his or her schooling from 11 years to 16 years. Many other possible cleavages, surprisingly, do not materialize. Industry of employment is not systematically related to trade policy preferences. Those working in "trade-exposed" industries (e.g., textiles and apparel) are not more likely than others to oppose freer trade. In views on immigration policy, location does not matter. People living in "immigration gateway" communities (e.g., California) are not more or less likely than others to oppose freer immigration. We do find some other differences in opinion: for example, union members are more likely to oppose freer trade, and blacks and immigrants are more likely to support freer immigration. And we do find evidence of issue linkage: proenvironment people are more likely to oppose freer trade, and individuals with generally more tolerant attitudes are more likely to support freer immigration. But across both

---

(2000). Destler (1995) provides a comprehensive overview of recent US trade politics. Baldwin and Magee (2000) examine the determinants of recent Congressional trade policy votes and, in consonance with our skills-preferences division, they find that the less skilled the labor force in a legislator's district, the more likely that legislator is to oppose trade bills.

6. We limit our analyses of cleavages in public preferences to trade and immigration, where we have, relative to FDI, much better data.

trade and immigration preferences, no other cleavage is as consistently important as that of labor-market skills. The main policy concern seems to be the perceived economywide labor-market pressures generated by liberalizations.

Note that this skills-preferences cleavage is a statement of central tendencies: all else being equal, individuals with more labor-market skills are more likely to support freer trade and immigration. But across many dimensions all else is not equal in the real world, and the other cleavages we describe matter as well. Thus, for many reasons—for example, issue linkage with environmental concerns—some highly skilled individuals can be expected to be skeptical of liberalizing policies. Also, note that our focus on skill differences across individuals runs solely along the dimension of labor-market abilities and is itself an admittedly imperfect measure. For empirical analysis of labor-market pressures, however, the skill measures we employ are thought to be the most accurate—or least imprecise—available. A critical point to keep in mind is that less-skilled workers, as typically defined by labor economists, constitute the majority of the US labor force.

These two key findings raise two questions. What sorts of labor-market *pressures* have been facing different skill groups in the US economy? What role has globalization played in these pressures? The answers are summarized below.

First, the premium earned by more-skilled American workers over less-skilled workers has been rising sharply since the late 1970s. Second, average real-wage growth in the United States has been sluggish since the early 1970s, the recent improvement of the past 5 years notwithstanding. All this means that *compared with high-skilled workers, the majority of the US labor force has had close to zero or even negative real-wage growth for about 25 years.* These patterns differ sharply from earlier decades, when real-wage growth was both faster and enjoyed by all groups, with steady or declining inequality.

Globalization appears to have had at least some role in these changes, as is suggested superficially by figures 1.1 through 1.3. On closer inspection, however, globalization's role seems to be only modest. Most academic research has concluded that increased trade, immigration, and FDI have not been the most important forces driving shifts in real and relative wages. Growth in labor productivity and real wages has been slowest in the service sectors, many of which are nontraded or are largely domestically owned. And technological change favoring skilled workers seems to have been the major force driving up the returns to skills. There is little evidence that greater trade, immigration, and FDI have played the main role in widening inequality, though they have played some.

Despite this balance of academic evidence, preferences about globalization policy divide strongly across labor-market skills, suggesting that globalization is perceived to be an important source of wage pressure. Surveys show people believe globalization has slowed real-wage growth and increased relative-wage inequality. In this book, we discuss this relationship between worker perceptions and pressures. For many reasons, it is important *not* to see the two as somehow inconsistent. First, a small effect of globalization on wages is not zero effect. Second, people may think government policy cannot impede technological change, so they may opt for antiglobalization policies. And third, people may be forward-looking: even if they think globalization has had no role in US labor markets so far, they may think it will in the future.

The book is organized as follows. Chapter 2 presents the public opinion evidence on US opposition to globalization. Chapter 3 presents some standard economic models to understand what opinion cleavages might underlie the surveys, and then presents empirical evidence on these divisions by documenting both the skills-preferences cleavage and the absence of other expected cleavages. Chapter 4 puts all this in the context of recent US labor-market pressures and their link to globalization. Chapter 5 concludes with a discussion of the links between worker preferences and pressures and of how our findings inform the policy debate about globalization.

2

Public Perceptions and Preferences about Globalization

When asked about trade, immigration, or foreign direct investment (FDI) policies, what do Americans think? This chapter shows that Americans display a qualitatively accurate appreciation of both the benefits and the costs of liberalization, but that a consistent plurality or majority tend to weigh the costs more heavily than the benefits and thus oppose liberalization.

In recent years public opinion surveys have paid increasing attention to globalization, asking more questions and covering more related subjects. Our analysis in this chapter is based on a database we assembled from the Public Opinion Databank at the Roper Center for Public Opinion Research covering more than 500 questions and answers dating back to 1938. Our goal is to present data from a representative sampling of surveys to set out "the facts" about US policy preferences and about what trade-offs seem to underlie these preferences.

In presenting this information, we use mainly recent survey questions and answers, given our interest in the current globalization backlash. Historical evidence is noted throughout and will be returned to in chapter 5. We also pay attention to language. Different surveys ask questions with different wording, and we try to examine these differences to better understand public opinion about globalization. As the reader will note, the majority of polling on globalization addresses trade only. Accordingly, we address trade questions first and in greater detail before turning to immigration and FDI.

The Facts about US Policy Preferences

Fact 1: Large majorities of Americans think that trade generates the benefits predicted by economics.

One way to gain insight on trade policy opinions is to examine whether Americans acknowledge the economic benefits and costs of freer trade. We start with the benefits. Economists argue that countries benefit from freer trade through consumption gains—in greater product variety and lower prices—and through production gains—by focusing resources on comparative-advantage industries and forcing firms to innovate and to set prices more competitively.

Do Americans think that trade actually generates these benefits? Overwhelmingly, yes. On the consumption side, nearly 90 percent of Americans think that trade increases product variety.

Question:	Because of imports from other countries, American consumers have a larger selection of goods and products to choose from.
Responses, 1999:	Strongly agree: 58% Somewhat agree: 26% Somewhat disagree: 8% Strongly disagree: 5% Undecided: 3%
Responses, 1998:	Strongly agree: 63% Somewhat agree: 26% Somewhat disagree: 6% Strongly disagree: 4% Undecided: 1%

Source: EPIC/MRA, April 1998 and May 1999

Over 60 percent of Americans think that they would face higher prices if forced to buy American-made goods only.

Question:	If you were to buy only American-made goods, do you think the cost of buying those goods would be more or less than you are currently paying now for those goods, or would you say it would be about the same price?
Responses:	Much more: 24% Somewhat more: 37% About the same: 27% Somewhat less: 9% Much less: 1% Undecided: 2%

Source: EPIC/MRA, April 1998

And about 70 percent of Americans think that trade lowers prices specifically for low-income families.

Question:	If it were not for less expensive products that are imported from other countries, many low-income American families would not be able to afford many of the products they are able to buy.
Responses, 1999:	Strongly agree: 46% Somewhat agree: 23% Somewhat disagree: 13% Strongly disagree: 13% Undecided: 5%
Responses, 1998:	Strongly agree: 47% Somewhat agree: 27% Somewhat disagree: 13% Strongly disagree: 10% Undecided: 3%

Source: EPIC/MRA, April 1998 and May 1999

As for trade's gains on the production side, about 75 percent of Americans think that trade induces greater innovation and price discipline from American manufacturers.

Question:	Imports from other countries keep American manufacturers on their toes and make them work harder to improve the quality and prices of their products to be more competitive.
Responses, 1999:	Strongly agree: 50% Somewhat agree: 23% Somewhat disagree: 15% Strongly disagree: 10% Undecided: 2%
Responses, 1998:	Strongly agree: 58% Somewhat agree: 25% Somewhat disagree: 7% Strongly disagree: 8% Undecided: 2%

Source: EPIC/MRA, April 1998 and May 1999

Beyond these traditional gains from trade, a majority of Americans also seem to grasp some other aspects of trade's role in the economy. For example, a majority of Americans agree that many jobs in largely non-traded industries depend on imports.

Question:	Some of the best high-paying jobs in transportation, banking, advertising, and design are jobs related to imports from other countries.
Responses:	Strongly agree: 26% Somewhat agree: 26% Somewhat disagree: 17% Strongly disagree: 13% Undecided: 18%

Source: EPIC/MRA, April 1998

Despite this evidence that people acknowledge the benefits of trade, it is less clear whether they think these gains arise for a country *unilaterally*— that is, regardless of whether other countries reduce their trade barriers. The following question suggests that a large majority of Americans think in a mercantilist fashion—generally assuming that running trade surpluses is beneficial and that trade protection is a good way to do so— believing that lower US trade barriers are a good idea only if other countries also lower their trade barriers.

Question:	Here are two statements. Tell me which one you most agree with. A: The US should lower its barriers even if other countries do not, because consumers can buy cheaper imports and foreign competition spurs American companies to be more efficient. B: The US should only lower its barriers if other countries do, because that is the only way to pressure them to open their markets.
Responses:	Statement A: 28.1% Statement B: 69.4% Don't know/refused: 2.5%

Source: Program on International Policy Attitudes, October 1999

Granted, this question could be interpreted in a less mercantilist, strategic manner. Those choosing statement B may believe that trade does generate unilateral gains, but may balance this against strategies for inducing foreign trade liberalization. In any event, subject to this mercantilist caveat, the large majority of Americans do acknowledge trade's benefits.[1]

---

1. There is historical evidence of widespread mercantilist attitudes as far back as the 1940s. In 1946, only 35 percent of Americans responded "a good thing" to the question "Do you think it would be a good thing for the United States, or a bad thing, if we reduced our tariffs on the goods that we buy from other countries?" (Another 35 percent responded "a bad thing," and 30 percent answered "don't know.") But when the other 65 percent were asked, "Do you think the United States should reduce its tariffs on goods that other countries want to sell here, providing they reduce their tariffs on goods we want to sell to them?" 73 percent responded "yes" (*Source:* National Opinion Research Center). Similarly phrased question-pairs in the 1950s yielded very similar responses. In interpreting these question-pairs, it is worth noting that public opinion scholars have observed a norm of "fair play" or "reciprocity" in individual attitudes about a wide variety of subjects (see Schuman and Presser [1981] for a detailed discussion).

Fact 2: A majority of Americans think that trade generates labor-market costs in job destruction and wage pressures.

What about the costs of international trade? Despite the economic gains Americans perceive from international trade, they also perceive there to be economic costs as well: wage pressures and job destruction. As for wages, a large majority of Americans think that trade, at least with low-wage countries, pressures American wages.

Question: Do you think that trade agreements with low-wage countries such as China and Mexico lead to higher or lower wages for Americans?

Responses: Higher wages: 19%
             Lower wages: 68%
             Don't know: 11%
             Refused: 2%

Source: Harris for *US News and World Report,* April 2000

Surveys have asked many more questions about whether trade destroys American jobs. When the issue is presented with just two options—trade either creates or destroys jobs—Americans are equally divided in their assessments.

Question: Do you think that expanded trade leads to an increase or decrease in the number of US jobs?

Responses: Increase in jobs: 45%
             Decrease in jobs: 44%
             Don't know: 10%
             Refused: 1%

Source: Harris for *US News and World Report,* April 2000

Question: Do you think expanded trade leads to an increase or a decrease in US jobs?

Responses: Increase in jobs: 37%
             Decrease in jobs: 56%
             Don't know: 7%

Source: Business Week/Harris, September 1997

Question: Do you think trade with other countries creates or loses more jobs for the US?

Responses: Creates more jobs: 39%
             Loses more jobs: 40%
             No effect on jobs: 11%
             Don't know: 10%

Source: CBS, February 1996

The following question decomposes trade into imports, assumed to destroy jobs, and exports, assumed to create jobs. Despite the different wording, people remain about equally split.

Question:	Do you think that more jobs are lost from imports or more jobs are gained from exports?
Responses:	More jobs lost from imports: 44.8% More jobs gained from exports: 45.8% No jobs lost or gained: 1.3% Don't know/refused: 8.1%

Source: Program on International Policy Attitudes, October 1999

When the issue is presented with the additional option of trade both creating and destroying jobs about equally, this additional option seems to be selected by the majority of those who would have responded that trade creates jobs. A plurality believes that trade destroys jobs.

Question:	Do you think trade agreements have mostly lost jobs or gained jobs for this country?
Responses, 1997:	Mostly lost jobs: 42% Done both about equally: 41% Mostly gained jobs: 7% Don't know: 10%
Responses, 1993:	Mostly lost jobs: 50% Done both about equally: 40% Mostly gained jobs: 4% Don't know: 6%

Source: CNN/*Time Magazine*, April 1997 and April 1993

When the issue is presented just in terms of imports destroying jobs, nearly 90 percent of respondents claim that imports destroy US jobs.

Question:	Do you think that importing foreign products means the loss of many jobs in this country, only a few jobs, or no jobs?
Responses:	Many jobs lost: 38.2% Only a few jobs lost: 49.7% No jobs lost: 9.1% Don't know: 2.8%

Source: Program on International Policy Attitudes, October 1999

If asked about the effect of trade on jobs in respondents' home communities, the same general split emerges: half claim little or no effect, but of the other half, three times as many cite more job destruction than job creation.

Question:	Have free-trade agreements done more to create or to cost jobs in your area?
Responses:	More to create jobs: 9%
	More to cost jobs: 30%
	Not much difference: 50%
	Don't know: 11%

Source: NBC News/*Wall Street Journal,* October 1998

Overall, this series of questions indicates widespread concerns about wage pressures or job destruction arising from trade. Do these concerns accord with economic theory? Yes and no.

As for wages, standard economic models predict that trade liberalization can hurt certain groups in society. The idea that freer trade benefits countries *on average* does not mean that freer trade benefits every *individual* within a country. We discuss this more in chapter 3.

As for job creation and destruction, in standard trade models trade is about the *kinds* of jobs in a country, not the *number* of jobs (see, e.g., Richardson and Rindal 1995; 1996). This is not to say that trade liberalization does not destroy jobs: it surely does. But in standard models, it is presumed that dislocated workers regain employment elsewhere in the economy. Thus, trade both destroys and creates jobs at the same time. Indeed, this reallocation of jobs according to patterns of comparative advantage is precisely how a country realizes aggregate gains from trade—without any net change in jobs. Clearly, one could argue that full-employment models assume away the possibility of unemployment. But in many other trade models that do not assume full employment, trade helps create jobs by providing a source of demand for a country's products beyond its own domestic demand.

How these issues of job destruction and creation are related to the above survey questions, unfortunately, is vague, because the questions do not distinguish gross and net flows. That said, the labor-market costs from trade—both the theory and empirical evidence on which groups may be hurt—will be a central part of the analysis in subsequent chapters. For now, we note that standard trade models do not characterize gross job destruction as a cost of trade, in the same way that gross job creation is not a benefit. But, undoubtedly, the general population's perceptions differ from those of economists. This is clear from the following question on jobs, which was asked of both the overall population and economists.[2]

---

2. Survey questions whose wording presumes trade-related job losses have been asked for decades. However, we found that this kind of wording became much more common in the early 1970s. This timing broadly coincides with adverse wage developments in the US labor market, which we will address in Chapter 4. Before the early 1970s, the majority of trade questions addressed issues of reciprocity, both in general and specifically regarding GATT agreements.

Question:	Do you think that trade agreements between the United States and other countries have helped create more jobs in the US, or have they cost the US jobs, or haven't they made much of a difference?

Responses from general public:
Cost jobs: 54%
Helped create jobs: 17%
Haven't made a difference: 27%
No opinion: 2%

Responses from economists:
Cost jobs: 5%
Helped create jobs: 50%
Haven't made a difference: 42%
No opinion: 3%

Source: Kaiser/*Washington Post*/Harvard Poll, July 1996

Fact 3: When asked a question that mentions both benefits and costs of trade, a plurality or majority of respondents choose the answer emphasizing the costs, not the benefits.

Having documented that most Americans perceive trade as having both benefits and costs, the obvious question is, what do Americans think about trade on balance? Do they think the benefits outweigh the costs, or vice versa? Do they want more or less trade liberalization? A large number of survey questions present both the pros and cons of trade and then ask respondents to state whether pros or cons matter more. Again, almost all economists think that trade generates net benefits. Most Americans seem to think otherwise. A large number of surveys show that, when asked a question mentioning both benefits and costs to trade, a plurality or majority of respondents choose the answer emphasizing the costs, not the benefits.

Here are five questions of the "trade is good or trade is bad" variety. Each makes a statement that trade is good for various reasons, follows with a statement that trade is bad for other reasons, and then asks which statement better accords with the respondent's opinions. In four cases more respondents pick bad over good; in the fifth, more pick good by only a small margin.

Question:	Now, I am going to read you two statements about foreign trade, and I would like you to tell me which statement best reflects your views on the issue.
	Statement A: Foreign trade is good for the US economy, resulting in economic growth and jobs for Americans.

Or, Statement B: Foreign trade is bad for the US economy, as cheap imports hurt wages and cost jobs.

Responses:
Good for the US economy: 34%
Bad for the US economy: 48%
Don't know: 18%

Source: NBC News/*Wall Street Journal*, April-May 2000

Question:
Please tell me which of the following two statements comes closer to your point of view. Free trade is a good idea, because it can lead to lower prices and the long-term growth of the economy. Or, Free trade is a bad idea, because it can lead to lower wages and people losing their jobs.

Responses:
Good idea: 50.9%
Bad idea: 44.2%
Don't know/refused: 4.9%

Source: Program on International Policy Attitudes, October 1999

Question:
Now, I am going to read you two statements about foreign trade, and I would like you to tell me which statement best reflects your views on the issue.
Statement A: Foreign trade has been good for the US economy, because demand for US products abroad has resulted in economic growth and jobs for Americans here at home.
Or, Statement B: Foreign trade has been bad for the US economy, because cheap imports from abroad have hurt wages and cost jobs here at home.

Responses:
Good for the US economy: 32%
Bad for the US economy: 58%
Some of both: 6%
Not sure: 4%

Source: NBC News/*Wall Street Journal*, December 1998

Question:
Now, I am going to read you two statements about foreign trade, and I would like you to tell me which statement best reflects your views on the issue. Statement A: Imports from abroad are, on the whole, good for the US because they make available more and cheaper goods for American consumers. Or, Statement B: Imports from abroad are, on the whole, bad for the US because they take away jobs and hurt wages of American workers.

Responses:
Good for the US: 33%
Bad for the US: 55%
Some of both/not sure: 12%

Source: NBC News/*Wall Street Journal*, September 1997

Question: Do you think that trade with other countries is bad because it has subjected American companies and employees to unfair competition and cheap labor, or good because it has opened up new markets for American products and resulted in more jobs?

Responses: Bad: 48%
                 Good: 42%
                 Not sure: 10%

Source: NBC News/*Wall Street Journal,* June 1997

The following question uses the phrase "the global economy" rather than trade, but it raises the same issues of many trade questions and again elicits a majority of negative responses.

Question: I'm going to read you some pairs of statements and ask you to choose which one comes closest to your point of view, even if neither is exactly right. The global economy will help average Americans because it will strengthen our economy and keep prices affordable for consumers, or the global economy will hurt average Americans because businesses will rely more on cheap labor from other countries and US jobs will be lost. Which comes closest to your point of view?

Responses: Global economy will help: 43%
                 Global economy will hurt: 52%
                 Don't know: 5%

Source: Pew, May 1999

The following question asks how people would vote in light of the pros and cons of trade. Among those answering, respondents are split in choosing between a trade-destroys-jobs candidate and a trade-creates-jobs candidate.

Question: Would you be more likely to vote for Candidate A, who says free trade would create high-paying jobs, or Candidate B, who says it would cause the loss of US jobs?

Responses: Candidate A: 44%
                 Candidate B: 45%
                 Not sure/no answer: 11%

Source: Hart and Teeter, September 1998

Other questions ask people about trade barriers: should they be implemented to ameliorate the negative aspects of trade, or not be implemented to allow the benefits from trade? In this first question, two-thirds of all respondents prefer tariffs to protect jobs and wages despite the cost of higher consumer prices.

Question: Now, I am going to read you two statements about foreign trade, and I would like you to tell me which statement best reflects your views on the issue.
Statement A: The United States should tax foreign goods imported into this country in order to protect American jobs and wages.
Or, Statement B: The United States should not tax foreign goods . . . because this will raise the prices American consumers will have to pay for these goods.

Responses: Should tax foreign goods: 66%
Should not tax foreign goods: 27%
Don't know: 7%

Source: CNN/*Time Magazine,* February 1996

Even more compelling time-series evidence comes from a *Los Angeles Times* survey conducted annually since 1982. Every year, approximately two-thirds of respondents have opted for a policy of trade barriers to protect jobs over a policy of free trade to allow broader consumer variety and lower consumer prices.

Question: Do you think it should be the policy of the United States to restrict foreign imports into this country to protect American industry and American jobs, or do you think there should be no restrictions on the sale of foreign products in the United States in order to permit the widest choice and lowest prices for the American consumer?

Responses, range from 1982 to 1997:
Restrictions: 63%-72%
No restrictions: 22%-28%
Don't know: 6%-10%

Source: Los Angeles Times, annually since 1982

The following question about freer trade is particularly revealing, as it focuses specifically on the issue of temporary (i.e., partial-equilibrium) job destruction induced by trade liberalization. It lays out a scenario that explicitly assumes both no net job destruction and no wage pressures— here new jobs pay more than old jobs. But a majority of respondents still oppose freer trade. This suggests that people are especially concerned about trade's job churning, even if it results in higher wages with no net employment losses.

Question:	As you may know, with freer trade, jobs are often lost due to imports from other countries, while new jobs are created when the US exports more products to other countries. I'd like you to imagine in one industry some jobs are lost because of foreign competition, while in a different industry an equal number are created, but these new jobs pay higher wages. Which of the following statements do you agree with the most?
	A: Even if the new jobs that come from freer trade pay higher wages, overall it is not worth all the disruption of people losing their jobs.
	B: It is better to have the higher-paying jobs, and the people who lost their jobs can eventually find new ones.
Responses:	Statement A: 55.5%
	Statement B: 40.3%
	Don't know/refused: 4.2%

Source: Program on International Policy Attitudes, October 1999

This persistent pattern of opting for trade barriers to protect jobs or wages also holds when Americans are asked about specific industries rather than about the overall economy. Here is a question about protecting the US steel industry, which lobbied Congress in 1999 for trade barriers in the face of sharply lower import prices from many Southeast Asian countries. Among those stating an opinion, the majority opted for protection.

Question:	In the wake of surging steel imports, Congress is considering legislation to protect the US steel industry and their workers from foreign competition. Opponents of the legislation say such action would make American steel companies less competitive, would encourage other countries to close their markets to our steel imports, and would violate internationally accepted trade rules. Do you think Congress should pass laws to protect US industry, or should US companies be exposed to global market competition?
Responses:	Congress should pass laws: 47%
	Companies should be exposed: 39%
	Not sure: 14%

Source: EPIC/MRA, May 1999

An even larger majority of Americans opt for trade protection for the clothing industry, with protecting jobs apparently more important than lowering prices.

Question:	Currently the US has numerous barriers, such as import taxes and quotas, that limit the amount of clothing imported into the US. There is some discussion about whether these barriers should be lowered. On the one hand, if the US lowered these barriers this would allow Americans to buy clothing at a much lower cost. On the other hand, lowering barriers would create competition for American clothing manufacturers and some American jobs would likely be lost. What is your opinion? Do you lean in favor of lowering or not lowering barriers that limit clothing imports?
Responses:	Lean toward lowering barriers: 35.7% Lean toward not lowering barriers: 62.0% Don't know/refused: 2.3%

Source: Program on International Policy Attitudes, October 1999

This clothing question was followed by an additional question with data on just how costly US trade barriers in clothing actually are: more than $50,000 per saved clothing industry job. This amount is nearly three times higher than the 1997 average wage in US apparel of about $18,400. Knowing the actual dollar cost of protection, nearly two-thirds of respondents still stated that this cost was worth it.

Question:	Some economic experts have calculated that having these barriers costs the American economy a substantial amount of money, mostly due to the higher prices consumers must pay. While the barriers may save jobs, these economists calculate that it costs the American economy more than $50,000 for EACH job saved. Assuming this is true, do you feel this cost to the American economy is worth it if it will save jobs, or is that too high a cost to save jobs? (*Asked only to those who responded "Lean toward not lowering barriers" in previous question*)
Responses:	Worth it: 65.1% Too high a cost: 28.2% Don't know/refused: 6.6%

Source: Program on International Policy Attitudes, October 1999

Here is another industry-specific question, for footwear, which quantifies the benefits of lower prices against the costs of lower wages (albeit with imaginary quantities). The same general message obtains: nearly two-thirds of respondents think that trade liberalization would be a mistake if it traded lower footwear wages for less expensive shoes.

Question:	Let's say there is an American factory making shoes that sell for about $70, and the workers there make about $28,000 a year. Then the US makes a trade agreement with a poorer country, so that their shoes can be imported into the US. These shoes sell for $50, saving American consumers $20. As a result of this competition the American shoe factory closes so the workers have to get new jobs. These jobs pay on average $23,000 a year—$5,000 less. Overall, would you think the US did the right thing or made a mistake by making the trade agreement?
Responses:	Did the right thing: 31.4% Made a mistake: 63.1% Don't know/refused: 5.5%

Source: Program on International Policy Attitudes, October 1999

Indeed, when directly asked if they would be willing to buy only American products and pay higher prices to protect American jobs from trade competition, at least a third of respondents support this idea—and in 1999, supporters were a larger share of respondents than objectors. Of those willing to pay more, the mean amount ranged between $40 and $50 per month. The 1998 mean amount works out to 1.5 percent of the average household real income that year ($38,885).[3]

Question:	Some people say they are willing to spend more to buy only American products because doing so protects American jobs. . . . How much more per month are you willing to include in your family budget to buy only American-made products and goods?
Responses, 1999:	Not willing to pay more: 31% Willing to pay more: 39% Mean amount: $40.71 Undecided: 30%
Responses, 1998:	Not willing to pay more: 41% Willing to pay more: 34% Mean amount: $48.34 Undecided: 25%

Source: EPIC/MRA, April 1998 and May 1999

To summarize Fact 3, a majority of the US public choose answers emphasizing costs of trade rather than benefits when asked questions explicitly referring to both.[4]

---

3. Of course, there may be a substantial difference between claiming willingness to pay more and actually paying more.

4. As mentioned earlier in note 2, survey questions whose wording presumes trade-related job losses became much more common in the early 1970s, around the time when important

Fact 4: When asked a trade policy question that does not mention trade's benefits and costs, a plurality or majority of respondents still oppose policies aimed at freer trade.

The previous section showed that across a wide range of questions that mention both benefits and costs of trade, a plurality or majority of respondents choose the answer emphasizing the costs, not the benefits. One might worry that the framing of these questions might somehow bias responses against trade. If simply asked about US trade policy without reference to any pros and cons, are Americans more inclined to support freer trade?

The answer is largely no. A number of surveys that do not address trade's benefits and costs find either that a plurality or majority of Americans oppose US policies aimed at freer trade or that opinion is equally divided. To start, here are some questions about US trade policy in general—questions not aimed at any particular piece of US legislation.

Questions about Overall US Trade Policy

The following broad question recently asked if Americans prefer free trade, fair trade, or trade protection.

Question:	Which of the following best describes your views about foreign trade? Do you consider yourself to be someone who believes in free trade or trade without any restrictions, someone who believes in fair trade or trade with some standards for labor and the environment, or someone who is protectionist, meaning that there should be rules to protect US markets and workers from imports?
Responses:	Free trader: 10% Fair trader: 51% Protectionist: 37% Don't know: 3%

Source: Harris for *US News and World Report,* April 2000

---

adverse wage patterns appeared in the US labor market. The phenomenon of plurality-to-majority protectionist responses goes back decades. We offer two comments on this time-series evidence. First, our reading of this evidence is that more-protectionist responses tend to be elicited by questions that presume that labor-market pressures are the downside of trade rather than some other economic issue, such as protecting industries. Second, our reading is that public opinion turned more protectionist after the early 1970s. In 1957, for example, high-tariff and low-tariff responses were split equally (at 34 percent) in response to the question "Do you think tariffs should be fairly high to protect people's jobs and our own industry from foreign competition, or should they be fairly low to keep prices down and encourage international trade?" (*Source:* Roper). From the early 1970s forward, questions like this usually elicited more protectionist responses than liberalizing responses. Other question frames before 1970 typically elicited even more pro-free trade responses (e.g., see notes 1 and 5).

For every American who self-identifies with free trade, nearly nine others support interventionist trade policies—with protectionists outnumbering free traders almost four to one. When the question about trade is phrased more starkly as a yes-or-no proposition, responses are split evenly.

Question: Please tell me if you strongly agree, somewhat agree, somewhat disagree, or strongly disagree with [the following statement]: 'Oppose free trade agreements.'

Responses: Strongly/somewhat agree: 44%
             Strongly/somewhat disagree: 45%
             Not sure: 11%

Source: Zogby for Reuters, April 1999

Other questions about support of free trade have been put in the context of the ongoing process of trade liberalization. This question asks what people think about the *pace* of this process.

Question: I would like to know how you feel about the process of increasing trade between countries through lowering trade barriers, such as taxes on imports. Do you feel this process has been going too fast, too slowly, or at about the right pace?

Responses: Much too fast: 12.6%
             A bit too fast: 17.3%
             At about the right pace: 38.9%
             A bit too slowly: 14.2%
             Much too slowly: 9.1%
             Don't know/refused: 7.9%

Source: Program on International Policy Attitudes, October 1999

Slightly more respondents think the pace has been too fast than too slow. This suggests that, looking forward, more people want liberalization to slow down rather than to speed up. This is indeed the case: in the following question, a plurality of respondents want US trade policy to slow or stop trade rather than allow it to continue or promote it.

Question: Overall, with regard to international trade, do you think that it should be the goal of the US to:

Responses: Try to actively promote it: 31.6%
             Simply allow it to continue: 25.9%
             Try to slow it down: 31.2%
             Try to stop or reverse it: 7.9%
             Don't know: 3.3%

Source: Program on International Policy Attitudes, October 1999

The previous questions were normative: Would people like the government to impede trade via protectionist policies? Surveys also contain a related descriptive question: Do people think the government actually can impede trade via protectionist policies? People might think that communication and transportation innovations make greater trade inevitable regardless of policy. But in fact, over 60 percent of Americans do think that protectionist policies can impede trade.[5]

Question: Do you think that it is possible for the government to stop or reverse the increase of international trade?

Responses: Yes: 61.4%
               No: 31.9%
               Depends: 4.8%
               Don't know: 1.9%

Source: Program on International Policy Attitudes, October 1999

Questions about US Trade Policy: China

As stated in chapter 1, in early 2000 the central US trade policy issue was whether to grant China permanent normal trading relations (PNTR). The China PNTR bill did pass Congress, but throughout the 1990s a widening majority of US citizens opposed granting China PNTR (PIPA 2000). Here are two examples of survey questions on China.[6]

Question: As you may know, the United States grants a trade status to most nations it trades with known as normal trade relations treatment. In your opinion, should the US grant this same status to China, or not?

Responses: Yes: 32%
               No: 54%
               Don't know/refused: 14%

Source: Pew Research Center, June 1999

---

5. For these broad trade-policy questions, like the pro-con trade questions discussed in note 4, our reading of the historical evidence is that public opinion turned more protectionist after the early 1970s. In 1961, 40 percent of respondents reported favoring lower US tariffs, versus only 31 percent favoring higher tariffs (*Source:* Gallup). But by 1978, high tariffs on US imports were favored by 47 percent of respondents but opposed by only 31 percent of respondents; the split grew to 50 percent versus 28 percent by 1981 (*Source:* Roper).

6. PIPA (2000, 48) also points out that opposition to Chinese PNTR rose even more when questions stated—inaccurately—that this policy would require lower US tariffs on Chinese imports. This finding is consistent with other mercantilist evidence.

Question: Do you think the United States should have free
trade with China on the same terms the US gives
its main trading partners, or not?

Responses: Yes: 44%
No: 46%
Don't know/refused: 10%

Source: ABC News, June 1998

Questions about US Trade Policy: NAFTA

Throughout the 1990s, a central US trade issue was the implementation
of the North American Free Trade Agreement (NAFTA). US citizens were
basically split over whether this trade agreement was good or bad for
the country (with a nontrivial minority unsure). Here are several examples
of this.

Question: Do you think the North American Free Trade
Agreement (NAFTA) has been good or bad for
the United States?

Responses: Good: 39%
Bad: 35%
Don't know/neither: 25%

Source: Harris, April 1999

Question: Has the North American Free Trade Agreement
(NAFTA) been good for the US?

Responses: Good: 37%
Bad: 47%
Don't know: 16%

Source: CNN/Gallup/*USA Today,* October 1998

Question: Has the North American Free Trade Agreement
(NAFTA) been a good or bad thing for the US?

Responses: Good thing: 39%
Bad thing: 39%
Don't know: 22%

Source: Los Angeles Times, September 1998

Question: What impact has the North American Free Trade
Agreement (NAFTA) had?

Responses: Negative: 29%
Positive: 23%
Not much: 32%
Don't know: 16%

Source: Hart and Teeter, September 1998

| Question: | Do you favor or oppose the North American Free Trade Agreement (NAFTA)? |

Responses: Favor: 42%
                Oppose: 36%
                Don't know/neither: 22%

Source: Business Week/Harris, September 1997

This ambivalence about NAFTA seems to translate into most Americans' opposing policies aimed at building on the NAFTA somehow. When a NAFTA question is rephrased from an evaluative question like those above to a forward-looking normative question, the majority of Americans do not want to continue with NAFTA as is. For the following question, in all three years, a plurality of respondents said they want to change NAFTA (in unspecified ways).

Question: After observing how NAFTA has worked between the United States, Mexico, and Canada over the past few years, do you think America should continue the NAFTA agreement, should America pull out of NAFTA, or should it be continued with changes?

Responses, 1999: Pull out of NAFTA: 18%
                  Continue NAFTA with changes: 40%
                  Continue NAFTA: 24%
                  Don't know: 18%

Responses, 1998: Pull out of NAFTA: 16%
                  Continue NAFTA with changes: 47%
                  Continue NAFTA: 23%
                  Don't know: 14%

Responses, 1997: Pull out of NAFTA: 17%
                  Continue NAFTA with changes: 30%
                  Continue NAFTA: 30%
                  Don't know: 23%

Source: EPIC-MRA, 1997-99

A majority of Americans oppose extending NAFTA to other countries in Latin America.

Question: Should the North American Free Trade Agreement (NAFTA) be extended to Latin America?

Responses: Yes: 34%
                 No: 54%
                 Don't know/neither: 12%

Source: Business Week/Harris, September 1997

And a majority of Americans oppose granting additional presidential authority to negotiate agreements like NAFTA.

Question:	Should Congress make it easier for the President to make pacts like NAFTA?
Responses:	Favor: 44% Oppose: 52% Don't know: 4%

Source: CNN/Gallup/*USA Today*, October 1998

Questions about US Trade Policy: Fast Track

In the latter 1990s, President Clinton was unable to secure renewal for fast-track negotiating authority. The majority of Americans have consistently opposed renewal. Here are three examples.

Question:	As you may know, President Clinton has asked Congress to give him 'fast-track' authority to negotiate free-trade agreements. The fast-track authority would mean that once negotiations are completed, Congress would take an up-or-down vote on an agreement as a whole, but could not vote to make any amendments or changes in the agreement. Do you strongly favor, somewhat favor, somewhat oppose, or strongly oppose having Congress grant the President fast-track authority to negotiate new free-trade agreements?
Responses:	Strongly favor: 21% Somewhat favor: 20% Somewhat oppose: 18% Strongly oppose: 31% Don't know: 10%

Source: CNN/Gallup/*USA Today*, October 1998

Question:	Should Congress renew 'fast track' authority?
Responses:	Yes: 36% No: 54% Don't know/neither: 10%

Source: Business Week/Harris, September 1997

Question:	As you may know, President Clinton has asked Congress to give him 'fast track' authority to negotiate more free trade agreements. The 'fast track' authority would mean that once the negotiations are completed, Congress would take an up-or-down vote on an agreement as a whole, but could not vote to make any amendments or changes in the agreement. Do you strongly favor, somewhat favor, somewhat oppose, or strongly

oppose having Congress grant the President 'fast track' authority to negotiate new free trade agreements?

Responses: Strongly favor: 10.0%
Somewhat favor: 21.9%
Somewhat oppose: 29.5%
Strongly oppose: 35.7%
Don't know/refused: 3.0%

Source: Program on International Policy Attitudes, October 1999

On fast track, many commentators pointed out that Americans are more likely to support policies (trade or otherwise) that maintain the status quo rather than initiate change. Indeed, for a time fast-track supporters were consciously using the phrase "normal negotiating authority" rather than "fast track." To examine this framing issue, PIPA re-asked a fast-track question with alternative language emphasizing fast track's historical precedent.

Question: Presidents since 1974 have had trade negotiating authority known as 'fast track,' which means the trade agreements the President negotiated are considered in Congress within 90 days and put to a simple yes or no vote, without any additions that could upset the agreement. The authority to do this expired in 1994, and President Clinton no longer has such authority. Do you strongly support renewing President Clinton's fast track trade authority, somewhat support, somewhat oppose, or strongly oppose it?

Responses: Strongly support: 14.0%
Somewhat support: 28.9%
Somewhat oppose: 24.1%
Strongly oppose: 31.3%
Don't know/refused: 1.8%

Source: Program on International Policy Attitudes, October 1999

Although the margin of opposition narrowed with this alternative wording, a majority of respondents still opposed renewing fast-track authority.

Fact 5: Respondents are more likely to support international trade when it is described broadly either without direct reference to US trade policy or without any reference to policy at all.

When trade is described in broader terms without direct reference to US policy, support is much stronger. Here is a question characterizing trade simply as market transactions.

Question: On balance, do you think trade with other coun-
                         tries—both buying and selling products—is
                         good for the US economy, or is it bad for the US
                         economy, or does it have no effect?

Responses: Good: 69%
                         Bad: 17%
                         No effect: 7%
                         Don't know: 7%

Source: CBS News, October 1996

Here is another example that refers to trade only without mentioning
policy. A plurality of respondents report trade to be positive, on balance.

Question: As you may know, international trade has
                         increased substantially in recent years. I would
                         like to know how positive or negative you think
                         the growth of international trade is, overall.
                         Please answer on a scale from 0 to 10, with 0
                         being completely negative, 10 being completely
                         positive, and 5 being equally positive and nega-
                         tive.

Responses: Above 5: 41%
                         5: 35%
                         Below 5: 20%
                         Don't know/refused: 4%
                         Mean: 5.51
                         Median: 5.50

Source: Program on International Policy Attitudes, October 1999

Even if trade is discussed in the context of policy, support also seems
higher when the question is phrased without direct reference to just the
United States but more vaguely to agreements in general.

Question: Overall, do you approve or disapprove of free
                         trade agreements with other countries?

Responses, 1999:   Approve: 60%
                         Disapprove: 26%
                         Undecided: 14%

Responses, 1998:   Approve: 59%
                         Disapprove: 26%
                         Undecided: 15%

Responses, 1997:   Approve: 61%
                         Disapprove: 24%
                         Undecided: 15%

Source: EPIC/MRA, 1997-99

This switch in opinions between questions about US trade agreements and questions about trade agreements more generally might reflect mercantilist attitudes. What might be going on is that Americans lend more support to trade agreements that require other countries to lower their trade barriers. Here is evidence to support this interpretation.

Question: The United States and China are negotiating a trade agreement that would lower Chinese tariffs on imports of US goods and remove other trade barriers. US companies are optimistic about the buying potential of China's huge market, as well as China's pledge to follow international trade rules. Do you think a trade agreement between China and the United States is in the best interests of the United States, or not?

Responses: Trade agreement is in US's best interests: 51%
Trade agreement is not in US's best interests: 34%
Undecided/don't know: 15%

Source: EPIC/MRA, May 1999

Unlike the questions about Chinese PNTR, this question finds a majority of respondents in support of a US trade agreement with China. What is different is that this question makes no reference to US trade liberalization. Instead it describes how the Chinese will lower their barriers to US goods; how US firms will gain greater access to the Chinese market; and how China will be compelled to follow rules—all classic mercantilist arguments.

Fact 6: A plurality or majority of Americans want fewer immigrants coming into the country, as Americans acknowledge some economic benefits of immigration but seem to worry more about perceived labor-market costs.

Public opinion about immigration broadly parallels that of trade. On the one hand, Americans acknowledge that immigrants generate economic benefits, such as more tax revenue thanks to their labor income (along with noneconomic benefits, such as cultural diversity).

Question: Do immigrants help improve our country with their different cultures and talents?

Responses: Yes: 69%
No: 28%
Don't know: 3%

Source: Gallup/*Newsweek,* August 1990

On the other hand, there is widespread concern about the effects immigration has on the labor market, in particular the perceived threat of immigrants taking jobs from American-born workers. The following question asks respondents whether immigrants "take jobs away" from people already in the United States. Again, the question does not specify whether respondents should consider the short term or the long term, but the large majority think that immigrants do take jobs—with a plurality responding that this outcome is extremely likely or very likely.

Question: The growing number of Hispanic immigrants [in the US economy]: How likely is it to take jobs away from people already here?

Responses: Extremely likely: 17.7%
                   Very likely: 25.6%
                   Somewhat likely: 33.2%
                   Not at all likely: 11.9%
                   Don't know/no answer: 11.6%

Source: National Election Studies Survey, 1992

Question: The growing number of Asian immigrants [in the US economy]: How likely is it to take jobs away from people already here?

Responses: Extremely likely: 16.7%
                   Very likely: 26.8%
                   Somewhat likely: 32.8%
                   Not at all likely: 11.9%
                   Don't know/no answer: 11.8%

Source: National Election Studies Survey, 1992

In light of these labor-market concerns, one might expect Americans not to support immigration liberalization when asked questions that highlight these concerns. This is indeed the case: a consistent plurality or majority feel that immigration should decrease. In response to the following question, which raises possible benefits and costs to immigration, over 70 percent of respondents opt for fewer immigrants, not more.

Question: Now, I am going to read you two statements about immigration, and I would like you to tell me which statement best reflects your views on the issue.
                   Statement A: Immigration should increase, to fill jobs companies have trouble filling.
                   Or, Statement B: Immigration should not increase, because it would cost US jobs and increase unemployment.

Responses: Immigration should increase: 20%
                   Immigration should decrease: 72%
                   Not sure: 8%

Source: NBC News/*Wall Street Journal*, December 1998

The same large coalition for less immigration also arises from broader questions that do not state costs and benefits, even when respondents are presented with the choice of keeping immigration at its current level. The following questions indicate that throughout the 1990s, fewer than 10 percent of Americans preferred any kind of increase in immigration.

Question:	Do you think the number of immigrants from foreign countries who are permitted to come to the United States to live should be increased a little, increased a lot, decreased a little, decreased a lot, or left the same as it is now?
Responses, 1996:	Increased a lot: 1.6% Increased a little: 3.1% Left the same: 32.9% Decreased a little: 26.5% Decreased a lot: 24.5% Don't know/no answer: 11.5%
Responses, 1994:	Increased a lot: 1.7% Increased a little: 3.5% Left the same: 28.2% Decreased a little: 21.9% Decreased a lot: 41.0% Don't know/no answer: 3.7%
Responses, 1992:	Increased a lot: 2.6% Increased a little: 5.1% Left the same: 41.6% Decreased a little: 24.5% Decreased a lot: 22.4% Don't know/no answer: 3.9%

Source: National Election Studies Survey, 1992, 1994, 1996

Fact 7: A majority of Americans want restrictions on both inward and outward foreign direct investment, as Americans acknowledge some economic benefits but seem to worry more about perceived labor-market costs.

Public opinion about FDI, both inward and outward, broadly parallels opinion about trade and immigration. There may be benefits to FDI, but people worry about its effects on the labor market and thus lean toward restrictive FDI policies. Let us start with inward FDI—foreign investment in the United States.

On the one hand, a plurality of Americans acknowledge that inward FDI generates economic benefits as foreign firms help invigorate US industry.

Question:	Do you agree or disagree: Foreign investment in the United States will help revitalize the US economy because it brings in new manufacturing processes, technology, and management techniques that can be learned by American employees?
Responses:	Agree: 49% Disagree: 43% Don't know: 8%

Source: Cambridge Reports/Research International, December 1990

On the other hand, there is significant concern about the effects inward FDI has on the labor market, especially whether it reduces the number of jobs. The following question does not specify whether respondents should consider the short term or the long term, but a plurality of respondents do think that FDI eliminates jobs.

Question:	On the whole, do you think foreign investment in the United States increases or decreases the number of jobs available to American workers?
Responses:	Increases: 36% Decreases: 47% Neither: 9% Don't know: 8%

Source: Cambridge Reports/Research International, January 1991

There also appears to be concern that inward FDI somehow grants foreigners excessive control over the US economy. Here is an example of this concern, revealed in a question weighing pros and cons of inward FDI. A majority of respondents think, on balance, that inward FDI is dangerous because it cedes too much control to foreigners.

Question:	There are different opinions about foreign investment in the US. Some people think that foreign investment is necessary and has a positive influence on our economy. Others say that foreign investment is dangerous because it allows outsiders too much control over our affairs. Which view is closer to your own?
Responses:	Necessary and positive: 42.7% Dangerous: 51.5% Don't know/refused: 5.8%

Source: Program on International Policy Attitudes, October 1999

In light of these labor-market and security concerns, one might expect Americans not to support FDI liberalization. This is indeed the case: the majority favor restrictions on inward FDI.

Question: Do you favor restricting foreign investments in
                   this country, or not?

Responses: Yes, favor: 59%
                   No, do not: 33%
                   Don't know/no answer: 8%

Source: Associated Press, November 1988

And, in keeping with the evidence that Americans are concerned about
the ownership implications as well as about the labor-market implications
of FDI, of the 59 percent who responded affirmatively to the above question, the large majority would restrict inward FDI even if such investment
created jobs.

Question: Would you feel that way (in favor of restricting
                   foreign direct investment in this country) even
                   if that foreign investment creates jobs for US
                   workers?

Responses: Yes, favor: 72%
                   No, do not: 22%
                   Don't know/no answer: 6%

Source: Associated Press, November 1988

With respect to outward FDI—US investment abroad—there is long-
standing and widespread concern among Americans that US companies
"export jobs" from the United States to foreign countries. In the following
question, almost 70 percent of respondents report being "really upset"
about this issue at least sometimes.

Question: I am going to read you a list of issues facing the
                   country. For each one, tell me how often you
                   personally really get upset about it—almost all
                   the time, a lot, sometimes, or almost never: . . .
                   'American companies building plants and creat-
                   ing jobs overseas.'

Responses: Almost all the time: 26%
                   A lot: 20%
                   Sometimes: 23%
                   Almost never: 30%

Source: Democrats for the 90s, February 1990

This degree of concern seems to imply that Americans believe that US
companies do export jobs and that doing so hurts the US economy. Over
90 percent of respondents cite job exports as a cause of US economic
difficulties.

Question: I am going to read you another list of reasons,
                       having to do with US businesses, that some peo-
                       ple have given for why the economy is not doing
                       better than it is. For each one, please tell me if
                       you think it is a major reason the economy is
                       not doing better than it is, a minor reason, or
                       not a reason at all. How about: 'companies are
                       sending jobs overseas?'

Responses: Major reason: 68%
                       Minor reason: 25%
                       Not a reason: 6%
                       Don't know/no opinion: 1%

Source: Washington Post, July 1996

This concern seems important enough that regardless of what gains
globalization might bring to American companies, a plurality or majority
of Americans think that companies moving operations overseas is a pre-
dominant feature of globalization.

Question: Which is closer to your view: America's integra-
                       tion in global markets spurs US companies to
                       develop new technologies and products, hone
                       their competitive edge, and create high-wage
                       jobs at home, or it encourages US companies to
                       move overseas to take advantage of low-wage
                       labor in developing countries?

Responses: Spurs companies: 40%
                       Encourages companies to move overseas: 50%
                       Don't know: 10%

Source: Democratic Leadership Council, July 1997

And when presented with policy options to limit overseas expansion by
US firms, a majority of Americans think that such policies would help
US workers.

Question: Let me read you some specific proposals about
                       things the government could do that might help
                       working families. . . . How much of a difference
                       would it make for working families if govern-
                       ment eliminated tax breaks for companies that
                       move US jobs overseas?

Responses: A great deal: 59%
                       Quite a bit: 11%
                       Just some: 12%
                       Very little: 13%
                       Not sure: 5%

Source: AFL-CIO, February 1997

Overall, this series of questions indicates widespread concern among Americans about inward and outward FDI destroying US jobs. However, standard economic models do not predict that FDI must destroy jobs in affected firms. Foreign firms obtaining US firms may alter initial employment levels—but the same is true of US firms obtaining other US firms, and in either case employment can rise, not just fall (such as in "greenfield" inward FDI, in which new business enterprises are constructed). Outward FDI can boost domestic employment (such as in "horizontal" outward FDI, which stimulates US parent company employment of parts suppliers, R&D scientists, and so on).

Beyond these ambiguous firm-level employment effects of FDI, in standard economic models the economywide number of jobs is unaffected by FDI. As with trade, FDI affects the kinds of jobs in a country, not the number of jobs, and realizing economywide gains from inward or outward FDI may require simultaneous job creation and destruction.

What about wages? As with trade, FDI may have effects on wages for certain labor groups. Rodrik (1997) contends that international capital mobility weakens the bargaining power of workers. When firms can threaten to relocate worldwide, workers feel greater wage pressure and also experience greater wage or employment volatility. That said, FDI can also boost wages (such as with inward FDI that brings better production technology for US workers).

How these issues of job destruction and creation are related to the FDI survey questions, unfortunately, is vague, because the questions do not distinguish gross and net flows of investment funds, nor do they mention effects of FDI on wages. We think it is important to interpret the survey evidence about FDI in light of these ambiguities.

Fact 8: American opinions about globalization are characterized by low amounts of information and by uncertainty, which is consistent with American opinions about most US policy issues.

Of course, individuals vary in how much they know about globalization issues and in how firmly they hold opinions on the subject. Many Americans, however, lack detailed knowledge about international trade, foreign direct investment, and immigration policies. This low amount of information is evident when respondents are asked direct questions about specific policy agreements. For example, near the height of congressional debate about normalizing trade relations with China, less than half of Americans had heard about this trade agreement.

Question:	The US and China reached an agreement that requires China to lower some of its trade barriers in return for membership in the World Trade Organization. Have you heard about this trade agreement or not?
Responses:	Yes: 46% No: 50% Don't know/refused: 4%

Source: Pew Research Center, May 2000

Furthermore, when given the option of responding "don't know enough to say" or "haven't thought much about it" to questions about trade policy, a sizable proportion of respondents choose this option. In one survey, nearly 40 percent of Americans said that they did not know enough to evaluate whether the Uruguay Round of the GATT would benefit the United States.[7]

Question:	As you may know, Congress recently approved a new world trade agreement called 'G.A.T.T.'— the General Agreement on Tariffs and Trade— which lowers world trade barriers and establishes an international organization that will have the power to rule on trade disputes between countries. Do you think G.A.T.T. will be good for the United States, bad for the United States, or don't you know enough about G.A.T.T. to say?
Responses:	Good: 42% Bad: 17% Don't know enough to say: 39% Not sure: 2%

Source: NBC News/*Wall Street Journal*, December 1994

Even when questions about trade, immigration, and foreign direct investment are framed more generally without reference to specific policies, the "don't know enough to say" or "haven't thought much about it" alternatives are sometimes chosen by nearly one-third of respondents. Many questions do not offer a "don't know" response option, but these questions still have as many as 10 percent of respondents declining to give an answer. This decrease in respondents declining to give an opinion when the option is not explicitly given suggests that even individuals who give an opinion in response to some questions are uncertain about it.

---

7. The lack of attention to the details of US trade policymaking seems to be true throughout the post-World War II era. For example, in 1947, a Gallup poll indicated that only 34 percent of respondents claimed to have heard or read about the international trade agreement establishing the GATT. Other polling evidence suggests that if anything awareness of international economic issues has increased as the US economy has become more integrated with the world.

Low information levels and uncertainty in public opinion are not, however, unique to the issue of globalization; they apply to US public opinion about most policy issues. To be sure, there is variation across policy issues. Even within the topic of globalization, individuals seem to have better-developed ideas about trade and immigration than they do about foreign direct investment. Nevertheless, there is consensus among public opinion scholars that levels of political and economic knowledge are low across most issues.[8]

Although globalization issues may not be remarkable on this information and uncertainty point, we acknowledge its importance in evaluating public opinion. In our view, this point does not imply that Americans lack meaningful, systematic opinions about globalization. On the contrary, we think that their opinions are coherent and reflect reasonable decisions rules.[9] Most people do not have an encyclopedic knowledge of policy options and of the workings of complex economic models. But as they gather information via work experiences, group affiliations, and the media, they can construct summary evaluations—albeit with error—broadly consistent with their interests and values.[10] Our empirical analysis in chapter 3 will test our contention that individuals have systematic, predictable opinions about globalization and will consider the implications of public information and uncertainty about these policies.

---

8. For examples of recent discussions about levels of political knowledge, see Zaller (1992), MacKuen, Erikson, and Stimson (1992), Delli Carpini and Keeter (1996), and Alvarez (1997).

9. The debate in the literature on the implications of low levels of information is very much an ongoing one. It begins with the minimalist perspective in which individuals are thought to have minimally consistent opinions based on limited information about and comprehension of political and economic issues (Converse 1964) and then proceeds with various revisions of this view (see, for example, Lane 1962; Key and Cummings 1966; Sullivan, Pierson, and Marcus 1978; Nie, Verba, and Petrocik 1979; Converse and Markus 1979; Conover and Feldman 1981; Zaller 1992; Delli Carpini and Keeter 1996). The most persuasive alternatives to minimalism can generally be described as low-information rationality models. A diverse set of analyses from this perspective (Downs 1957; Key and Cummings 1966; Kramer 1971; Alt 1979, 1991; Fiorina 1981; Chappell and Keech 1985; Conover, Feldman, and Knight 1987; Popkin 1991; Sniderman, Brody, and Tetlock 1991; MacKuen, Erikson, and Stimson 1992; Lupia 1992, 1994; Rahn, Aldrich, and Borgida 1994; Alvarez 1997; Lupia and McCubbins 1998; Sekhon 1999) emphasize—with many important distinctions—that despite the fact that individual citizens typically lack detailed information about politics, their opinions are coherent and reflect reasonable decisions rules.

10. Here is an example, which offers a preview of our analysis in chapter 3. The Stolper-Samuelson theorem predicts that trade liberalization alters a country's wages along factor lines, not industry lines, such that liberalization affects even workers in nontraded sectors. The adjustment process is quite complicated, hinging crucially on the idea of intersectoral factor mobility. To perceive wage pressures from trade liberalization, workers in construction need not know all the details of this theorem. It can be enough for them to see that a lot of the workers recently laid off from the town's apparel factory, closed as a result of import competition, are now applying for construction jobs.

Summary

We have presented a large amount of public opinion data here, but with a rather striking consensus. There is substantial skepticism about whether the net effects of economic globalization are positive, with pluralities or majorities of US citizens opposing policies to further liberalize trade, immigration, and foreign direct investment. Here are the key features of US public opinion about economic globalization that we have highlighted:

■ A large majority of Americans think that international trade generates the benefits that economic theory predicts.

■ However, a majority of Americans also worry that international trade generates labor-market costs in terms of job destruction and lower wages.

■ When asked a survey question that mentions both benefits and costs of international trade, a plurality or majority of respondents choose the answer that emphasizes the costs, not the benefits.

■ When asked a different kind of question that does not mention trade's benefits and costs, a plurality or majority of respondents still oppose policies aimed at freer trade.

■ The strongest support for international trade appears in response to questions that describe trade in broad terms, either without direct reference to US trade policy or without any reference to trade policy at all.

■ A plurality or majority of Americans want fewer immigrants coming into the country, as Americans acknowledge some economic benefits but seem to worry more about perceived labor-market costs.

■ A majority of Americans want restrictions on both inward and outward foreign direct investment, as Americans recognize some economic benefits but seem to worry more about perceived labor-market costs.

■ American opinions about globalization are characterized by low levels of information and by uncertainty, which is consistent with American opinions about most US policy issues.

This list is certainly not an exhaustive description of US public opinion about globalization. For example, we did not address public opinion linkages between the economic dimension of globalization and other dimensions, such as human rights and the environment. These additional elements of public opinion are interesting, and we will address some of them in the remainder of the book. We also did not examine in this chapter the idea that public support for liberalization may be sensitive to the degree to which liberalization is linked to adjustment policies addressing the costs borne by individual workers. This aspect of public opinion is important and we present some evidence consistent with this argument in the book's conclusion.

In this chapter, rather, we sought to present an accurate and comprehensive portrait of US preferences about the main economic issues at stake in the globalization debate. The next two chapters will analyze these preferences in two complementary ways: first, by examining what opinion cleavages (if any) underlie them, and second, by putting them in the context of recent US labor-market performance.

3

Cleavages in Public Preferences about Globalization

Given the evidence presented in chapter 2 on preferences about globalization policies, an important question to explore is whether any opinion cleavages underlie them. There may be none; subgroups across demographic, geographic, political, or other lines may have broadly similar opinions. Alternatively, there may be clear constituencies that tend to support or oppose globalization. As discussed in chapter 1, identifying such cleavages will provide a richer understanding of Americans' preferences about globalization. In this chapter we focus on opinions about trade and immigration policy. We first outline some theory about possible cleavages, and then turn to our data analysis.

Theory of Policy Preferences

In this section we briefly discuss some standard economic models of policy preferences that organize our empirical analysis. We seek to explain why some individuals might support certain types of globalization while others are likely to be in opposition. As with much of the literature on the political economy of trade and immigration policy, we assume that individuals evaluate policies on the basis of individual welfare, not aggregate national welfare—that is, of self-interest. The assumption is that

---

Much of the material in this chapter comes from Scheve and Slaughter (2001a, b). For a more complete discussion of many of the issues in this chapter, the reader is referred to those earlier works.

people care about how policies affect them personally, without regard for the policies' national effects. Further, we assume that personal welfare depends on current labor income. We acknowledge that welfare may also depend on other economic elements, such as asset ownership, as well as on noneconomic considerations. In our data analysis we will examine these other elements, both to provide a more complete understanding of opinion cleavages and to verify the robustness of any labor-market divisions that might emerge.

For simplicity, our theoretical discussion makes two additional assumptions. First, individuals know with certainty the effects policies have or will have on their incomes. This is a common but not universal assumption in the literature: individuals may or may not know beforehand how policy changes will affect their welfare (see, e.g., Fernandez and Rodrik 1991). Second, we assume full employment. In reality, some people are not in the labor force, and some in the labor force are not employed. Appendix A covers theoretical topics like these in greater detail, and we will also revisit them in our empirical analysis.

With these assumptions made explicit, it follows that the general form of our explanation of why some individuals prefer liberalization while others do not is quite simply that people support policy alternatives that improve the incomes they earn in the labor market. To identify which policies are beneficial to which individuals, we need to turn to economic theories about the relationship between policies and labor income.

Trade Policy and Income

Standard trade theory predicts that trade's effect on people's current income depends on the degree of intersectoral factor mobility or the degree of factor specificity—that is, the extent to which labor, capital, or any other input into the production of goods and services that individuals own can move about, or be moved about, among industries. The factor of production that is the focus of our discussion is labor. So, factor mobility refers to how easily individual workers can employ their skills across different industries. There are two main models to consider. In a Heckscher-Ohlin (HO) framework, where factors—in this case, workers—can move costlessly across sectors or industries, factor incomes—that is, labor wages and other income—tend to vary by factor type—that is, by different categories of workers. In contrast, in a Ricardo-Viner (RV) framework, where some or all factors cannot move to other sectors, factor incomes tend to vary by industry. Because factor mobility increases over time, it is often thought the HO model better describes longer time horizons, whereas the RV model better describes shorter ones.[1]

---

1. Many studies have examined how an RV short-run equilibrium transforms over time into an HO long-run equilibrium. See, for example, Mussa (1978) and Neary (1978).

In both models, changes in trade policy affect factor incomes by changing the country's product prices. The HO assumption that factors can move costlessly across sectors means that each factor earns the same return in all industries. In this model—again, assuming the factors in question are different kinds of labor—trade liberalization tends to raise wages for the types of workers that are employed relatively intensively in sectors whose relative prices are rising, and to lower wages for the types of workers employed relatively intensively where relative prices are falling (per the Stolper-Samuelson theorem, 1941).

This process works via cross-industry shifts in labor demand. Suppose international trade changes domestic product prices—for example, because of changes in US trade barriers (e.g., the United States eliminates apparel quotas in the Multifiber Arrangement) or because of changes in supply and demand in world markets (e.g., world apparel prices decline as China produces more). Whatever the case, at initial wages any industry enjoying a rise in its product price now earns positive profits, and any industry suffering a fall in its price now earns negative profits. Profit-maximizing firms respond by trying to increase output in profitable sectors and reduce output in unprofitable sectors. As firms do this, economy-wide demand for different kinds of labor changes. Relative labor demand increases for the types of workers that are employed relatively intensively in expanding sectors and reduces for the workers intensively employed in the contracting sectors. For equilibrium to be restored, at fixed labor supply, relative wages for the different types of workers must adjust in response to the demand shifts until profit opportunities are arbitraged away.

Note that in the HO framework, it is not just people working in traded industries—industries engaged in trade—who face wage pressures from international trade. Workers in nontraded industries do too, not directly through international product-market competition, but indirectly through domestic labor-market competition. Thus if US trade barriers in apparel were removed, it would not just be American apparel workers who would face wage changes. It would be all workers in the US economy competing in the same labor market as these apparel workers—whatever industry they work in.

So what predictions does the HO framework make about opinion cleavages on US trade policy? First, we must specify what exactly we mean by different types of workers. Economists typically distinguish types in terms of "human capital", i.e., a wide set of on-the-job skills (literacy, numeracy, problem-solving ability, etc.). Empirically, worker skills are usually measured via educational attainment, occupation classification, or employment experience. Second, it is necessary to make an assumption about which sectors of the economy receive trade protection. For the HO framework, it is usually assumed that the government of the country in question extends trade protection to the sectors that employ relatively intensively the factors of production—for our purposes, different skill groups of workers—in which the country is poorly endowed relative to the rest of the world, because in the country's opening from autarky to free trade, these workers undergo income declines. In contrast, the workers with which the country is well endowed relative to the rest of the world undergo income gains in the opening from autarky to free trade. Thus the types of workers that a country has in abundant supply support freer trade, and its scarce types of workers oppose it—regardless of industry of employment.

Many studies (e.g., Leamer 1984) have shown that the United States is well endowed with more-skilled labor relative to the rest of the world. And in recent decades, the US pattern of trade protection, at least for tariffs in manufacturing, accords with the model's predictions: US tariffs throughout the 1970s and 1980s were higher in less-skill-intensive industries (Haskel and Slaughter 2000). According to the HO model, US workers with relatively more skills should support freer trade, and those with less skills should be more likely to oppose it.

The RV model, by contrast, assumes that some or even all types of labor cannot move across sectors, thanks to mobility barriers such as industry-specific human capital gained through workers' on-the-job experience. These immobile, or specific, workers need not earn the same return in all sectors. Instead, their income is linked to their sector of employment as trade liberalization-induced changes in relative product prices redistribute income across sectors rather than across different types of labor. Sectors whose product prices fall—presumably sectors with comparative disadvantage—realize income losses for their workers, and sectors whose product prices rise—presumably sectors with comparative advantage—realize income gains for their workers. Thus if trade liberalization lowers the US domestic price of apparel, then workers specific to that sector, regardless of what type of workers they are—that is, what their skill levels are—suffer income declines.

In the RV model, trade policy preferences are determined by sector of employment. Workers employed in sectors with product prices elevated by trade protection should oppose trade liberalization, and workers employed in sectors with prices lowered by protection should support it. What about the preferences of workers in nontraded industries? Unlike in the HO model, here workers in nontraded industries are insulated from international product-market competition to the extent that domestic prices of nontraded goods, by definition, are not directly affected by trade pressures. But insofar as freer trade raises national income, if income elasticities of demand for nontraded goods are positive, then freer trade should raise prices of nontraded goods by raising demand for them. So in an RV model, workers in nontraded sectors support freer trade, but perhaps less than do workers in sectors that have comparative advantage, because trade policy's effect on prices of nontraded goods works indirectly through demand for those goods.[2]

Immigration Policy and Income

To make the connection between individual factor income and immigration policy preferences, we briefly summarize three models: the HO trade model, the factor-proportions-analysis model, and the area-analysis model.[3] For all three models, we assume that US citizens know that current immigrant inflows increase the relative supply of less-skilled workers. This assumption clearly reflects the facts about US immigration in recent decades (see, e.g., Borjas et al. 1997). It implies that preferences depend on how an immigration-induced shift in US relative labor supply toward less-skilled workers affects factor incomes. For simplicity we assume just two factors of production, more-skilled and less-skilled labor.

The HO trade model usually assumes interregional labor mobility as well as the intersectoral labor mobility discussed above, which means that there are no geographically segmented "local" labor markets. The wage effects of immigration depend on the magnitude of the immigration shock and on whether the country's economy is large enough to have any influence on world product prices.

In the HO framework, immigrant inflows sometimes have no wage effects at all; immigrants are completely absorbed via changes in output mix. With the change in supplies of more- and less-skilled workers available to hire, firms have an incentive to produce more of those products that employ relatively intensively the now more-abundant less-skilled workers (per the Rybczynski theorem, 1955). Thanks to trade, these output changes can be absorbed into world markets, and if the country is too small for this absorption to affect world prices, then its wages do not change either. The long-run nature of the HO model is crucial here, as changes in output mix take time.

But in the HO framework, immigrant inflows sometimes do change wages. For example, if the country is sufficiently large, then its output changes do alter world prices and thus wages (via the Stolper-Samuelson process). Or if the immigration shock is sufficiently large, then firms have an incentive to start up entirely new industries, which means that

---

2. If some factors remain mobile across sectors in a Ricardo-Viner model, their factor prices are not so clearly linked to product-price changes. Changes in real factor prices for these mobile factors are ambiguous: the direction of change depends on the consumption basket of these mobile factors. In the above discussion we focus only on the specific factors.

3. The terms "area analysis" and "factor-proportions analysis" come from Borjas et al. (1996).

absorption entails changes in both output and wages. In either case, less-skilled wages fall relative to more-skilled wages.

Thus the HO model has different predictions about the link between skill levels and immigration policy preferences. If individuals think that immigration does not alter wages, then there should be no link between skill levels and preferences. In this case, people evaluate immigration on the basis of other considerations. If individuals think that immigration affects wages, then less-skilled workers nationwide should prefer policies that lower immigration inflows, and more-skilled workers nationwide should prefer policies that raise immigration inflows.

Like the HO model, the factor-proportions-analysis model also assumes a national labor market. But unlike the HO model, it assumes a single aggregate output sector. This means that there can be no changes in output mix to absorb immigrants. Instead immigrants price themselves into employment via lower wages. Any immigration inflow affects national wages as one might expect without changes in output mix: less-skilled immigrants accept lower wages to induce firms to hire them. The larger the immigrant inflow, the larger the wage changes.

This model makes a single prediction about the link between skill levels and immigration policy preferences: Less-skilled workers nationwide should prefer policies that lower immigration inflows, and more-skilled workers nationwide should prefer policies that raise immigration inflows. Note that this prediction can also come from the HO model.

Like the previous model, the area-analysis model also assumes a single output sector. However, it assumes distinct, geographically segmented labor markets within a country. For countries like the United States that have a great deal of internal migration, this assumption is probably inappropriate in the very long run. It may be realistic over shorter time spans, however, thanks to frictions such as information and transportation costs that people must incur to move. The more important these frictions are, the more sensible it is to treat Portland, Maine, and Portland, Oregon, as two distinct labor markets. Hence economists often analyze "local" labor markets within the United States, usually defined by states, cities, or metropolitan areas (e.g., the Twin Cities of Minneapolis and St. Paul plus surrounding suburbs). Each local market has its own equilibrium wages determined by local supply and local demand.

In this framework, how do Americans think about the labor-market effects of immigration? Well, it depends on where immigrants settle. If there is literally no mobility between local labor markets, then immigrants pressure wages only in the "gateway" communities where they arrive—and it is well documented that immigrants are indeed concentrated in these gateway communities. In 1990, 75 percent of all immigrants residing in the United States lived in one of six gateway states: California, Florida, Illinois, New Jersey, New York, and Texas. Borjas et al. (1996) report that in 1992, 60 percent of all US legal immigrants came into California or New York alone; another 20 percent entered the other four gateway states.

What does this framework predict for immigration policy preferences? In the area-analysis model, less-skilled workers in gateway communities should prefer policies that lower immigration inflows, and more-skilled workers should prefer policies that raise inflows. In nongateway communities there should be no correlation between workers' skill levels and their preferences. More generally, with some labor mobility, similarly skilled workers everywhere should have the same preferences, but the link between skill levels and preferences should be stronger among workers in gateway communities. Less-skilled workers in gateway communities should have stronger preferences for more restrictive immigration policies than less-skilled workers in non-gateway communities, and more-skilled workers in gateway communities should have stronger preferences for less restrictive immigration policies than more-skilled workers in non-gateway communities.

Summary

We have sketched out a number of possible opinion cleavages under the assumption that people evaluate trade and immigration policy on the basis of how policy alternatives impact their labor income. Trade policy preferences may cleave along skill levels—as measured by education or income—and along industry of employment. Immigration policy preferences may cleave along skill levels and geography. Further, different cleavages may hold over different time horizons, as sectoral or geographic labor mobility increases over time. In light of these predictions, we now turn to the data.

Data Description

We analyzed data from the 1992, 1994, and 1996 National Election Studies (NES) surveys (Sapiro et al. 1998), each of which is an extensive survey of current political opinions based on an individual-level stratified random sample of the US population. The NES surveys contain direct measures of individual preferences about trade and immigration policy.

These surveys also record a wealth of respondent information such as educational attainment, occupation, industry of employment, and county of residence. With this information, we built data sets with several plausible measures of "exposure" to freer trade and immigration across different types of workers, industries, counties, and many other demographic and political control variables such as age, gender, ideology, and race. Merging this information with the NES survey data yielded individual-level data sets identifying both stated policy preferences and potential trade and immigration exposure through several channels. We then evaluated how these preferences vary with the individual characteristics that might matter, as predicted by the theories we reviewed in the previous section.

Here is the NES survey question about trade policy preferences:[4] "Some people have suggested placing new limits on foreign imports in order to protect American jobs. Others say that such limits would raise consumer prices and hurt American exports. Do you favor or oppose placing new limits on imports, or haven't you thought much about this?" This question requires respondents to reveal their general position on the proper direction for US trade policy. Note that the question does not mention what sector(s) would receive import restrictions. We assume that respondents think that import limits will be placed on sectors that have comparative disadvantage. This assumption seems sensible and plausible, and it allows us to construct measures of individual trade exposure that follow closely from the theory. We constructed the dichotomous variable *Trade Opinion* by coding responses of those individuals favoring protection as 1 and of those opposing it as 0.

Here is the NES survey question about immigration policy preferences: "Do you think the number of immigrants from foreign countries who are permitted to come to the United States to live should be increased a little, increased a lot, decreased a little, decreased a lot, or left the same as it is now?" This question requires respondents to reveal their general position on the proper direction for US immigration policy. Note that the question does not ask what skill mix immigrants would have relative to natives. We assume that respondents think that immigrant inflows would increase the relative supply of less-skilled workers. As discussed in the previous section, this assumption clearly reflects the facts about US immigration in recent decades.[5] We constructed the variable *Immigration Opinion* by coding responses of those individuals responding "decreased a lot" as 5, and so on down to 1 for those responding "increased a lot." Thus, higher scores on *Immigration Opinion* indicate preferences for more restrictive policy.

We then merged data for these survey questions with measures of trade and immigration exposure, in consonance with the hypotheses outlined in the previous section (see appendix B for further details about variable construction). To test whether skill levels are a key determinant of policy preferences, for each individual-year observation we constructed two variables measuring skill levels. One was *Education Years*, recorded in the

---

4. This question was not asked in the 1994 NES survey, so our trade analysis is limited to 1992 and 1996 data.

5. We recognize that this assumption abstracts from other interesting facts about the distribution of the skill levels of US immigrants. For example, Borjas et al. (1997, 7) show that the skill distribution of US immigration has concentrations at both the high-skill and low-skill ends of the distribution.

NES survey as years of education completed. The other was *Occupation Wage*, which was that year's average weekly wage nationwide for the three-digit Census Occupation Code occupation recorded for the individual. Educational attainment is a common skills measure; *Occupation Wage* assumes that average national earnings for a given occupation are determined primarily by the skills required for that occupation. According to the HO model, individuals with less education or in lower-wage occupations are more likely to benefit from trade restrictions on sectors that have a comparative disadvantage and thus are more likely to support new trade barriers.

To test whether sector of employment matters for trade policy preferences, for each person we constructed two measures of their industry's trade exposure. Each was based on the individual's recorded industry of employment coded according to the 1980 Census Industry Code classification. The first, *Sector Net Export Share*, is the industry's 1992 net exports (i.e., exports minus imports) as a share of its output. This variable follows the common assumption that an industry's comparative advantage is reflected in its net exports: industries that have positive net exports are assumed to have comparative advantage, and industries that have negative net exports are assumed to have comparative disadvantage. This variable covers manufacturing, agriculture, and tradable services; for all nontradable services industries, we set this variable equal to zero.

The second measure is the industry's 1992 US tariff rate, *Sector Tariff*, constructed as tariff duties collected as a share of customs-value imports. We assume that industries with higher values for *Sector Tariff* have more of a comparative disadvantage. The tariff data cover all tradable industries in agriculture and manufacturing; for all other sectors, we set this variable equal to zero. For both measures, according to the RV model, workers in industries with greater revealed comparative disadvantage are more likely to support trade protection for these industries.

For immigration policy preferences, we already have the individual skills measures *Education Years* and *Occupation Wage*. Examining whether immigration preferences vary across regions by immigrant inflows requires measures of where respondents live combined with information about gateway communities. For each respondent, the NES surveys record the county, state, and (where appropriate) metropolitan statistical area (MSA) of residence. We combined this information with immigration data to construct several alternative measures of residence in a high-immigration area. Below, results are reported for the dichotomous variable *High-Immigration MSA*, equal to 1 for residents living in a county or MSA where at least 10 percent of the 1990 population was immigrants (versus 7.9 percent for the overall population).

For the analyses of both trade and immigration preferences, we also constructed several measures of possible noneconomic determinants of

Table 3.1 Summary statistics for analysis of trade policy preferences

Variable	1992	1996
Trade Opinion	0.671	0.534
	(0.470)	(0.499)
Occupation Wage	0.532	0.652
	(0.187)	(0.231)
Education Years	13.288	13.872
	(2.610)	(2.554)
Sector Tariff	0.006	0.006
	(0.019)	(0.019)
Sector Net Export Share	− 0.004	− 0.001
	(0.091)	(0.092)
Observations	1,736	846

Note: These summary statistics are multiple imputation estimates based on the 10 imputed data sets for each year. Each cell reports the variable mean and (in parentheses) its standard deviation. *Trade Opinion* records people's responses to the question, "Some people have suggested placing new limits on foreign imports in order to protect American jobs. Others say that such limits would raise consumer prices and hurt American exports. Do you favor or oppose placing new limits on imports?" This is a dichotomous variable, which codes responses of those individuals favoring protection as 1 and of those opposing it as 0. *Occupation Wage* is the actual nominal weekly wage divided by 1,000.

preferences. These measures include variables such as gender, age, race, ethnicity, personal immigrant status, party identification, and political ideology. The precise definitions for these variables may be found in appendix B.

Table 3.1 reports summary statistics of our trade opinion measure and our key trade exposure variables.[6] Note that in 1992, about 67 percent of respondents favored trade restrictions and 33 percent opposed them. In 1996, among those giving an opinion, preferences were more evenly divided, with 53 percent supporting restrictions and 47 percent opposed. The averages reported in table 3.1 are very similar to national means obtained from other data sources. Table 3.2 reports summary statistics of our immigration opinion measure and our key immigration exposure variables. The "average" value for *Immigration Opinion* over the three surveys was about 3.8, between the responses "left the same as it is now" and "decreased a little," though closest to "decreased a little."[7]

---

6. These estimates and all the statistical analyses in this chapter rely on multiple imputation to address missing data problems. These procedures are explained in detail in appendix C.

7. Note that tables 3.1 and 3.2 indicate that the trade and immigration analyses are based on a different number of observations. This resulted from our decision not to impute answers

Table 3.2 Summary statistics for analysis of immigration policy preferences

Variable	1992	1994	1996
Immigration Opinion	3.595	3.982	3.785
	(1.027)	(1.064)	(0.982)
Occupation Wage	0.512	0.574	0.601
	(0.187)	(0.227)	(0.225)
Education Years	12.923	13.153	13.323
	(2.815)	(2.637)	(2.660)
High-Immigration MSA	0.235	0.227	0.215
	(0.424)	(0.419)	(0.411)
Observations	2,485	1,795	1,714

MSA = metropolitan statistical area.

Note: These summary statistics are multiple imputation estimates based on the 10 imputed data sets for each year. Each cell reports the variable mean and (in parentheses) its standard deviation. *Immigration Opinion* records people's responses to the question, "Do you think the number of immigrants from foreign countries who are permitted to come to the United States to live should be increased a little, increased a lot, decreased a little, decreased a lot, or left the same as it is now?" This variable codes responses of those individuals responding "decreased a lot" as 5, and so on down to 1 for those responding "increased a lot." *Occupation Wage* reports the actual nominal weekly wage divided by 1,000.

Econometric Specifications

For trade policy preferences, our empirical work aims to test how different types of trade exposure affect the probability that an individual supports trade restrictions. Again, *Trade Opinion* is coded 1 for those who support trade restrictions and 0 for those opposed. We model the variation in these zero-one responses using a familiar logistic form, which assumes that responses vary with a set of individual-specific explanatory variables hypothesized to affect the probability of supporting trade restrictions. We estimate the effect of these explanatory variables using logistic regressions.[8]

---

for those individuals who responded to the trade question "haven't you thought much about this." This specification decision is discussed in appendix C, and alternative approaches are discussed below. All the findings reported in this chapter are robust to alternative treatments of this response category as well as to alternative approaches for dealing with missing data generally in both the trade and immigration analyses.

8. Let $E(\textit{Trade Opinion}_i) = \Pr(\textit{Trade Opinion}_i = 1 \mid \pi_i) = \pi_i$, where i indexes each observation and π_i equals the probability that an individual supports trade restrictions. We model the variation in π_i according to a logistic form given by

$$\pi_i = \frac{1}{1+\exp(-x_i\beta)}.$$

The theory discussed earlier suggests alternative sets of explanatory variables to include in the analysis. Our baseline cases include eight different models. Each of the first four models includes just one of the skill or industry trade-exposure regressors. Models 5 through 8 test pairs of explanatory variables, one measuring skill levels and the other industry trade exposure. Each year of data is analyzed separately to allow for any differences across years. Specifications of these models employing alternative measures of trade exposure, using noneconomic variables, and estimating alternative econometric models are discussed below.

For immigration policy preferences, the empirical work also aims to test how skill levels affect the probability that an individual supports a certain level of legal immigration. The level of immigration a respondent prefers could theoretically take on any value, but the NES surveys record only which of five ordered categories the respondent chose. There is no strong reason to believe *ex ante* that these five categories are separated by equal intervals, so a linear regression model might produce biased estimates. The familiar appropriate model for this situation is an ordered probit, which estimates not only a set of parameters measuring the strength of explanatory variables but also additional parameters representing unobserved category thresholds.

Given these considerations, we estimated ordered probit models where the expected mean of the unobserved preferred immigration level is hypothesized to be a linear function of the respondent's skill level, a vector of demographic identifiers, political orientation, and (perhaps) the immigration concentration in the respondent's community.[9] The key hypothesis is whether more-skilled individuals are less likely to support restrictive immigration policies, as predicted in the HO trade model and in the factor-proportions-analysis model. Accordingly, the baseline specifications regress stated immigration policy preferences on skill levels, demographic identifiers, and political orientation. In a second set of specifications, we also included a zero-one variable indicating whether or not the respondent lives in a high-immigration area and an interaction term between this indicator and the respondent's skill level. These second

---

In this equation, x_i is a vector of individual-specific explanatory variables hypothesized to affect the probability of supporting trade restrictions, and β is a vector of effect parameters. Our standard errors on these parameter estimates are White robust standard errors to account for heteroskedasticity.

9. Our analyses of trade and immigration opinions employ control variables such as demographic identifiers and measures of political orientation. For the trade analysis, these variables are not included in the baseline analyses but are employed in the robustness checks presented below. For the immigration analysis, findings in previous studies of immigration opinions suggested inclusion of the control variables even in the baseline models (Citrin et al. 1997; Espenshade and Hempstead 1996). The skills findings presented below for both trade and immigration are robust to inclusion or exclusion of the controls.

Table 3.3 Determinants of individual opinion on international trade restrictions, 1992

Variable	Model 1	Model 2	Model 3	Model 4	Model 5	Model 6	Model 7	Model 8
Constant	1.642	3.648	0.696	0.711	1.625	1.642	3.651	3.650
	(0.168)	(0.350)	(0.054)	(0.051)	(0.170)	(0.168)	(0.355)	(0.351)
Occupation Wage	−1.716				−1.711	−1.720		
	(0.288)				(0.288)	(0.288)		
Education Years		−0.217					−0.217	−0.217
		(0.025)					(0.025)	(0.025)
Sector Tariff			2.730		2.420		−0.137	
			(2.994)		(3.089)		(2.976)	
Sector Net Export Share				−0.697		−0.720		0.027
				(0.612)		(0.614)		(0.615)

Note: These results are multiple imputation estimates of logit coefficients, with 1,736 observations for each of the 10 imputed data sets based on the 1992 NES survey data. Each cell reports the coefficient estimate and (in parentheses) its standard error. The dependent variable is individual opinions about US trade policy, a dichotomous variable defined such that 1 indicates preferences favoring trade restrictions and 0 indicates opposition.

specifications test whether the skills-immigration correlation is strongest in high-immigration labor markets, as in the area-analysis model. Again, each year of data is analyzed separately to allow for any differences across years.

Empirical Results: Do Skill Levels Affect Trade Policy Preferences?

The results of our logistic regressions for models 1 through 8 strongly support the hypothesis that individuals' skill levels—as measured by education and income—determine trade policy preferences. Little evidence is found consistent with the hypothesis that a person's industry of employment influences policy preferences.

The parameter estimates and their standard errors from models 1 through 8 for the 1992 and 1996 data are reported in tables 3.3 and 3.4. However, these coefficient estimates alone do not answer the key substantive question of how changes in skill levels and industry trade exposure affect the probability that an individual will support trade restrictions. To answer this question, the estimates from the regression models can be used to conduct simulations calculating the effect on the probability that an individual supports trade restrictions of changing one

Table 3.4 Determinants of individual opinion on international trade restrictions, 1996

Variable	Model 1	Model 2	Model 3	Model 4	Model 5	Model 6	Model 7	Model 8
Constant	1.625	4.031	0.084	0.137	1.555	1.610	4.028	4.063
	(0.240)	(0.519)	(0.073)	(0.069)	(0.245)	(0.242)	(0.540)	(0.529)
Occupation	−2.280				−2.232	−2.257		
Wage	(0.353)				(0.355)	(0.356)		
Education		−0.279					−0.278	−0.281
Years		(0.036)					(0.037)	(0.037)
Sector Tariff			8.885		6.401		0.124	
			(4.242)		(3.918)		(4.357)	
Sector Net				−1.180		−0.518		0.294
Export Share				(0.858)		(0.795)		(0.810)

Note: These results are multiple imputation estimates of logit coefficients with 846 observations for each of the 10 imputed data sets based on the 1996 NES survey data. Each cell reports the coefficient estimate and (in parentheses) its standard error. The dependent variable is individual opinions about US trade policy, a dichotomous variable defined such that 1 indicates preferences favoring trade restrictions and 0 indicates opposition.

variable from a typical below-average value to a typical above-average value while holding the other variables constant at their means.[10]

Tables 3.5 and 3.6 report the simulation results for models 5 through 8 for the 1992 and the 1996 data. Each row lists the estimated effect on the probability of supporting trade restrictions of an increase in that row's variable from one standard deviation below its sample mean to one standard deviation above, with all other variables held constant at their means. For example, the 1992 results from model 5 indicate that

10. This simulation procedure is best described with reference to a specific model and variable of interest. Consider model 5 and *Occupation Wage* (this model's other regressor is *Sector Tariff*) for the 1992 analysis. Recognizing that the parameters reported for this model are estimated with uncertainty, we drew 1,000 simulated sets of parameters from their sampling distribution (defined as a multivariate normal distribution with the mean equal to the maximum likelihood parameter estimates and the variance equal to the variance-covariance matrix of these estimates). For each of the 1,000 simulated sets of coefficients we then calculated two probabilities. First, we calculated the estimated probability of supporting trade restrictions when *Occupation Wage* is equal to one standard deviation below its mean and *Sector Tariff* is equal to its mean. Second, we calculated the estimated probability of supporting trade restrictions when *Occupation Wage* is one standard deviation above its mean and *Sector Tariff* is held at its mean. The difference between these two estimated probabilities is the estimated difference in the probability of supporting trade restrictions between an individual whose skill level is one standard deviation below the mean and an individual whose skill level is one standard deviation above the mean. We calculated this difference 1,000 times, and then, to show the distribution of this difference, we calculated its mean, its standard error, and a 90 percent confidence interval around the mean.

Table 3.5 Change in probability of supporting trade restrictions as a result of a two-standard-deviation increase in the independent variable for each model, 1992

Variable	Model 5	Model 6	Model 7	Model 8
Occupation Wage	−0.139 (0.023) [−0.178, −0.101]	−0.140 (0.022) [−0.175, −0.101]		
Education Years			−0.251 (0.025) [−0.293, −0.211]	−0.251 (0.026) [−0.293, −0.208]
Sector Tariff	0.014 (0.017) [−0.013, 0.042]		−0.001 (0.004) [−0.006, 0.006]	
Sector Net Export Share		−0.016 (0.014) [−0.039, 0.007]		0.000 (0.003) [−0.005, 0.005]

Note: For models 5 through 8, we estimated using multiple imputation with a logit specification the effect of factor and industry exposure to international trade on individuals' trade policy opinions. The parameter estimates from this analysis are reported in table 3.3. Here we interpret those results by presenting the impact of a two-standard-deviation increase in each independent variable, holding other variables constant, on the probability that the respondent supports trade restrictions. Each triplet of entries in the table begins with the mean effect from 1,000 simulations of the change in probability of supporting trade restrictions due to an increase from one standard deviation below the independent variable's mean to one standard deviation above it, with all other variables held constant at their means. The standard error of this estimate is then reported in parentheses, and the 90 percent confidence interval for the probability change is presented in brackets.

increasing *Occupational Wage* from one standard deviation below its mean ($345 per week), indicating a worker with below-average skill levels, to one standard deviation above its mean ($719 per week), indicating a worker with above-average skill levels, reduces the probability of supporting trade restrictions by 0.139 on average (standard error, 0.023; 90 percent confidence interval, −0.178 to −0.101).

Across all models in tables 3.5 and 3.6, higher skill levels are strongly correlated with lower probabilities of supporting trade restrictions. The mean estimates of probability changes are substantively significant and much larger in absolute value than those for the industry measures. They are also precisely estimated: all have 90 percent confidence intervals less than zero. In other words, these two tables indicate that if you could put a high school dropout with roughly 11 years of education (10.7 years in 1992, 11.3 years in 1996) through both high school and college, ending up with about 16 years of education (15.9 years in 1992, 16.5 years in 1996), then the probability that this individual supports trade protection would fall by some 25 to 35 percentage points.

Table 3.6 Change in probability of supporting trade restrictions as a result of a two-standard-deviation increase in the independent variable for each model, 1996

Variable	Model 5	Model 6	Model 7	Model 8
Occupation Wage	−0.244 (0.037) [−0.305, −0.184]	−0.247 (0.036) [−0.303, −0.183]		
Education Years			−0.344 (0.039) [−0.411, −0.281]	−0.346 (0.040) [−0.412, −0.282]
Sector Tariff	0.036 (0.022) [0.002, 0.075]		0.001 (0.004) [−0.005, 0.007]	
Sector Net Export Share		−0.011 (0.017) [−0.043, 0.016]		0.001 (0.003) [−0.004, 0.005]

Note: For models 5 through 8, we estimated using multiple imputation with a logit specification the effect of factor and industry exposure to international trade on individuals' trade policy opinions. The parameter estimates from this analysis are reported in table 3.4. Here we interpret those results by presenting the impact of a two-standard-deviation increase in each independent variable, with other variables held constant, on the probability that the respondent supports trade restrictions. Each triplet of entries in the table begins with the mean effect from 1,000 simulations of the change in probability of supporting trade restrictions due to an increase from one standard deviation below the independent variable's mean to one standard deviation above it, with all other variables held constant at their means. The standard error of this estimate is then reported in parentheses, and the 90 percent confidence interval for the probability change is presented in brackets.

In contrast, higher industry trade exposure has much more ambiguous effects. In the bivariate regressions reported in tables 3.3 and 3.4 (models 3 and 4), greater industry trade exposure is correlated with support for trade restrictions, but the estimated effects are statistically significant only for the *Sector Tariff* measure in 1996. Adding the skills measure *Occupation Wage* in models 5 and 6 produces qualitatively similar results. The 1992 and 1996 results for models 7 and 8, which include the skills measure *Education Years*, indicate that neither of the industry measures has a systematic relationship with the probability of supporting trade restrictions. And inspection of table 3.6 reveals that even for the one case in which a trade exposure variable has a marginally statistically significant effect (model 5, 1996), the substantive impact is quite small: a two-standard-deviation increase in *Sector Tariff* results in just a 0.036 increase in the probability of supporting trade restrictions.

Overall, comparing the industry results in tables 3.5 and 3.6 for models 5 and 6 with models 7 and 8, one cannot conclude with a high degree of confidence that individuals employed in relatively trade-exposed sectors are more likely to support trade restrictions.

The key message of the analyses presented in tables 3.3 through 3.6 is that an individual's skill level rather than industry of employment is strongly correlated with the probability of supporting trade restrictions. The effects of skill levels are large and precise; the effects of industry trade exposure are small and uncertain. These results suggest that people's concern about trade policy is consistent with the HO model, and that intersectoral labor mobility is relatively high in the United States over the time horizons relevant to individuals when they are evaluating trade policy.

Robustness Checks for Trade Policy Preferences

An initial check of the robustness of the trade policy findings is whether the results hold when other regressors are included in the analysis. We added a standard set of demographic and political control variables— measures for age, gender, race, political party identification, and ideology. These are standard control variables in opinion studies and may highlight other cleavages in public opinion about trade policy. These variables might account for variation in individual opinions that are based both on economic concerns in addition to the skills cleavage and on noneconomic considerations.[11]

Table 3.7 reports the results of these regressions for models 5 through 8 for the 1992 and 1996 data. The most important point to take away from this table is that the findings for the skills and industry measures are robust to the inclusion of these control variables. The skills parameters are remarkably stable and remain statistically and substantively significant. In contrast, the industry estimates are always insignificantly different from zero. In these models, skill levels rather than industry of employment explain individual opinions about trade. As for the control variables, for these specifications age and race do not have a consistently significant effect, and women and those who identify with the Democratic Party have systematically more protectionist opinions. The results for political

---

11. We include the political variables with some caution. To the extent that party identification and political ideology are in part determined by individuals' trade policy positions, including these measures as exogenous independent variables is inappropriate and could bias toward zero our estimates of any skills effect. The alternative view, and the reason to include party identification and political ideology in these regressions, is that trade and immigration may be difficult policy areas for individuals to have strong opinions about. Consequently, people may adopt their opinions largely on the basis of their view of themselves as "Democrats" or as "Republicans" and of what elites with those same labels say about trade and immigration policy.

Table 3.7 Determinants of individual opinion on international trade restrictions: Additional control variables

Variable	1992				1996			
	Model 5	Model 6	Model 7	Model 8	Model 5	Model 6	Model 7	Model 8
Constant	1.644	1.668	3.506	3.529	0.888	0.975	2.804	2.900
	(0.297)	(0.295)	(0.440)	(0.437)	(0.391)	(0.387)	(0.621)	(0.610)
Occupation Wage	−1.422	−1.440			−1.799	−1.842		
	(0.303)	(0.302)			(0.367)	(0.369)		
Education Years			−0.207	−0.208			−0.237	−0.243
			(0.026)	(0.026)			(0.039)	(0.039)
Sector Tariff	3.296		1.120		6.715		2.050	
	(3.316)		(3.260)		(4.480)		(4.690)	
Sector Net Export Share		−0.646		0.014		−0.341		0.391
		(0.619)		(0.626)		(0.898)		(0.828)
Gender	0.220	0.210	0.298	0.293	0.502	0.478	0.602	0.593
	(0.109)	(0.108)	(0.109)	(0.108)	(0.155)	(0.154)	(0.153)	(0.153)
Age 18-29	−0.079	−0.080	0.177	0.177	−0.400	−0.431	−0.139	−0.146
	(0.170)	(0.170)	(0.172)	(0.172)	(0.265)	(0.266)	(0.265)	(0.266)
Age 30-44	−0.242	−0.242	0.032	0.032	−0.652	−0.666	−0.393	−0.387
	(0.143)	(0.143)	(0.148)	(0.148)	(0.193)	(0.192)	(0.198)	(0.198)
Age 45-59	−0.164	−0.161	0.050	0.051	−0.594	−0.613	−0.327	−0.326
	(0.156)	(0.156)	(0.163)	(0.163)	(0.209)	(0.208)	(0.215)	(0.215)
Race	0.161	0.159	0.160	0.158	0.441	0.463	0.445	0.451
	(0.167)	(0.167)	(0.175)	(0.176)	(0.330)	(0.328)	(0.339)	(0.337)
Party Identification	−0.095	−0.094	−0.065	−0.064	−0.155	−0.154	−0.139	−0.140
	(0.030)	(0.030)	(0.031)	(0.031)	(0.045)	(0.045)	(0.046)	(0.047)
Ideology	−0.003	−0.001	−0.034	−0.034	0.273	0.273	0.260	0.263
	(0.044)	(0.044)	(0.046)	(0.046)	(0.069)	(0.070)	(0.070)	(0.071)
Observations	1,736	1,736	1,736	1,736	846	846	846	846

Note: These results are multiple imputation estimates of logit coefficients. Each cell reports the coefficient estimate and (in parentheses) its standard error. The dependent variable is individual opinions about US trade policy, a dichotomous variable defined such that 1 indicates preferences favoring trade restrictions and 0 indicates opposition.

ideology differ in the two years analyzed. In the 1996 survey, more-conservative respondents were more protectionist, all else being equal, but no relationship between ideology and opinions is evident in the 1992 data.

In addition to this standard set of control variables, we conducted further analyses including considerations that might reasonably be expected to influence individual opinions about trade. These analyses are useful both to check the robustness of our skills findings and to investigate other potentially interesting opinion cleavages about trade policy. Perhaps the most obvious such variable is trade union membership. We found that union members are, all else equal, more likely to favor new trade barriers. This relationship is estimated quite precisely for the 1992 data but less so in 1996. Including trade union membership does not substantially change any of the findings for the skills and industry measures.

Given the salience of issue linkage in descriptions of interest-group politics about globalization, it seems reasonable to explore how attitudes about other policy areas affect trade policy opinions among the general public. We focus in particular on how environmental opinions may influence support for additional trade barriers. The 1996 NES survey asked a number of questions measuring individuals' environmental concerns. From these questions we constructed two measures of each respondent's environmental preferences. We then added each of these measures individually and jointly to models 1 through 8 with and without the demographic controls. Although individuals who were more concerned about the environment were, as expected, more likely to support trade barriers, the effect was generally small and dependent on coding and specification choices. Moreover, regardless of the measure employed, in no specifications was the skills-preferences relationship significantly attenuated. Although concerns about the environment may have a role in describing interest-group politics about globalization, they do not seem to play a major part in public opinion about liberalization in the United States.

Another consideration that might affect individual opinions about trade policy is political awareness. Zaller (1992) and other public opinion scholars have shown that the extent to which individuals pay attention to and understand political and economic debate in the media may influence their opinions about many issues. Although a thorough evaluation of the impact of political awareness on individuals' opinions about trade is well beyond the scope of this book, it is useful to consider some of the most obvious ways in which political awareness might affect opinions about trade.

One possible effect is that individuals who are more politically aware may be more likely to be influenced by the near unanimity among economists that freer trade has net benefits. Thus individuals who are more aware and knowledgeable about political matters may, all else equal, be less likely to support trade restrictions. Although this is a reasonable hypothesis, we make it with some caution, as the consensus among economists does not extend to all elites with access to the media. We explore this particular hypothesis about political awareness because it can be restated as an alternative interpretation of our skills-preferences findings. Perhaps more-skilled individuals are simply more politically attentive and knowledgeable and thus, reflecting the consensus among economists, have more liberal attitudes about trade.

A second possible effect of political awareness is that it influences the variability of individual opinions about trade. As we showed in chapter 2, there is clear evidence of uncertainty in attitudes about globalization generally. The public opinion literature suggests that individuals with higher levels of awareness may, for some issues, have less variable opinions. Ignoring this possible source of heteroskedasticity (i.e., variability of preferences that itself varies systematically with the awareness of the individuals in our observations) might produce poor-fitting models that affect our inferences about the relationship between skill levels and opinion.

We tested these two hypotheses jointly by constructing a measure of political awareness for each respondent of the 1996 NES survey and by employing an alternative econometric model. Following Zaller (1992), our measure of political awareness is based on tests of neutral factual information about politics (e.g., "What job or political office does Al Gore hold? William Rehnquist? Boris Yeltsin?"). We included this measure of political awareness in each of our eight baseline regression models. Further, rather than estimating logit regressions with robust standard errors as in the previous analyses, we employed heteroskedastic probit models. These specify both a mean function for which we estimate the effect of various independent variables on the probability of supporting trade restrictions (as was the case in the logit analyses) and a variance function for which we estimate the effect of various measures on the variance of trade opinions.[12]

The results of this analysis are consistent with expectations. Individuals who are more attentive and knowledgeable about politics are, all else equal, less likely to support new trade restrictions. Moreover, their opinions about trade are also less variable. Accounting for these simple effects of political awareness does not substantially affect our skills and industry findings. Individual skill type is robustly correlated with trade opinion, and industry trade exposure is not.[13]

---

12. See Alvarez and Brehm (1995; 1997) for details about heteroskedastic probit models in studies of public opinion.

13. The results are also, of course, robust to simply adding the political-awareness measure to the original logit specifications. Including this variable does result in a modest attenuation in the estimated magnitude of the effect of skill type on the probability of supporting trade restrictions. In addition to the robustness checks discussed in this section, we conducted a

Asset Ownership and Trade Policy Preferences

The discussion so far in this chapter has focused on making the connection between individual economic welfare and policy opinions. Economic welfare in our analysis has thus far been limited to labor-market outcomes. Individuals, however, may consider dimensions of economic welfare above and beyond the effects of policy on labor income. The models outlined earlier in the theoretical section do not focus on *intertemporal* consumption choices, which allow current income to be saved and invested for future periods. In reality people do save and invest in a wide range of assets. Accordingly, it is worth discussing how policy preferences might be related to asset ownership. We focus our discussion of assets and policy preferences on trade.

Many kinds of assets fit easily into standard trade models. Some do not, however, because they are neither currently employed factors of production nor currently produced goods. An important example is residential housing. Firms do not employ houses as factors of production. And at each point in time, other than new construction nearly all of a region's housing stock is not produced: rather, it is the accumulation of all previous housing construction in earlier periods. Some assets, then, are not clearly linked to the production side of standard trade models. We focus on housing because it is the only asset of this kind recorded in the NES survey data. Note, however, that housing also constitutes a large share of people's total wealth holdings.

To understand how trade policy can affect housing prices, suppose a country has many distinct regional housing markets, each of which faces

---

number of alternative analyses to further verify our findings. To check the strength of our data we tried other measures of factor type and industry exposure. For factor type we tried the respondents' reported annual income. The results were qualitatively similar to those obtained for average occupation wages and education; we prefer the latter because they better reflect an individual's long-run earnings capacity, as annual income can fluctuate for reasons unrelated to skill levels such as illness, inheritances, and overtime. For industry trade exposure we tried imports as a share of output. Although imports do not measure revealed comparative advantage, imports are so often considered to be harmful that we thought many individuals might focus on imports only when evaluating trade policy. This import measure did not work as hypothesized, however. We also considered the possibility that the proper unit of observation is the household rather than the individual. The NES survey reports education, occupation, and industry of employment for spouses of respondents, so in some specifications we used regressors reporting a combination of respondent and spousal information. These household results were generally consistent with the individual results. Similar to the possible objection discussed above based on the hypothesized effects of political awareness, one might wonder whether the skills-preferences correlation reflects considerations other than labor-market pressures. One empirical result supporting the skills-preferences interpretation is that both *Occupation Wage* and *Education Years* are significant when placed in the regression together. If one variable is thought to measure something other than returns to skills, the significance of the other variable conditional on the first supports our interpretation.

a perfectly inelastic supply schedule at each point in time. Prices are then set by regional housing demand. As discussed by Caplin et al. (1997), a key driver of demand is the level of regional economic activity: more activity means more employment and more housing demand. Trade policy is one of the forces affecting the level of regional economic activity. Freer trade tends to shrink industries with comparative disadvantage and expand those with comparative advantage. Accordingly, regions with a higher concentration of activity in sectors with a comparative disadvantage are more vulnerable to adverse housing demand shocks from freer trade. As regional economic output declines, people leave the local labor force, either for work elsewhere or, at least temporarily, unemployment. These departures reduce housing demand and thus housing prices. Note that this trade-housing linkage operates whether the underlying factor markets follow the HO or the RV model. (See appendix A for further discussion.)

To summarize: We hypothesized that in regions with a greater concentration of activity in sectors with comparative disadvantage, homeowners would oppose freer trade because it tends to reduce their welfare by lowering regional housing demand and thus housing values.

To examine whether housing values matter for trade policy preferences, for each individual in the 1992 data we constructed two measures of the degree to which homeowners are exposed to trade liberalization. First, using NES survey data on respondent homeownership, we created the dichotomous variable *House*, coded 1 to indicate ownership and 0 otherwise. Next, using NES data on county of residence, we constructed two measures of county-level trade exposure. *County Exposure 1* measures the share of county employment accounted for by the 10 two-digit SIC manufacturing industries with above-median tariff rates in 1992. *County Exposure 2* measures the share of county employment accounted for by the 14 net-import industries in 1992. These two variables measure each county's employment in sectors with comparative disadvantage, identified through tariff rates or net trade flows. Our two measures of homeowner exposure to trade liberalization are the two interaction variables, *County Exposure 1* × *House* and *County Exposure 2* × *House*. We added these interaction terms and the county exposure variables to our baseline models to see if homeowners exposed to trade liberalization were more likely to oppose freer trade when the effects of trade policy on labor income were held constant.

The results of these analyses are consistent with our theoretical expectations (for details about variable construction and results, see Scheve and Slaughter 2001a). For the 1992 NES data, we estimate that for homeowners, an increase in county trade exposure from its sample mean to one standard deviation above its mean increases the probability of supporting trade restrictions by 0.029 to 0.039 (county exposure has no effect on those who are not homeowners). The results are estimated precisely and are very similar for *County Exposure 1* and *County Exposure 2*. There is clear evidence that homeowners living in counties with a larger share of employment in sectors with comparative disadvantage are more likely to oppose trade liberalization. This seems to be because regional housing values depend, among other things, on the amount of regional economic employment in trade-exposed sectors. These results suggest a further connection between individual economic welfare and public opinion about trade policy. In addition to current labor income driving preferences as in standard trade models, preferences also depend on asset values.

Empirical Results: Do Skill Levels Affect Immigration Policy Preferences?

Both the HO and factor-proportions-analysis models predict a skills-preferences cleavage on immigration policy opinion. Table 3.8 tests for this cleavage. It presents the results for each year's full sample, where in model 1 we measure skills with *Occupation Wage* and in model 2 we use *Education Years*. The key message of table 3.8, as indicated by the precisely estimated coefficients for *Occupation Wage* and *Education Years*, is that by either measure, skill levels are significantly correlated with *Immigration Opinion*. Less-skilled people prefer more restrictive immigration policy, and more-skilled people prefer less restrictive immigration policy.

This skills-preferences link is evident controlling for a large set of plausible noneconomic determinants of *Immigration Opinion*. Among these other regressors, *Gender*, *Age*, *Hispanic*, and *Party Identification* are insignificantly different from zero (although *Hispanic* is estimated to have a negative and statistically significant effect in 1994). *Race* and *Immigrant* are mostly significantly negative: blacks and the group of immigrants plus children of immigrants are more likely to prefer less restrictive immigration policy. *Ideology* is significantly positive: more conservative people are more likely to prefer more restrictive immigration policy. Our nonskills estimates are similar to those in Citrin et al. (1997) and Espenshade and Hempstead (1996); we report them for comparability.

The coefficient estimates in table 3.8 identify the qualitative effect on *Immigration Opinion* of skill levels and our other regressors. To answer our key substantive question of how *changes* in skill levels affect the probability that an individual supports immigration restrictions, we used the estimates of models 1 and 2 to conduct simulations calculating the effect on immigration preferences of changing skill levels while holding the other variables constant at their sample means. These simulations calculated the estimated probability of supporting immigration restrictions (i.e., the probability of supporting a reduction in immigration by either "a lot" or "a little") when a regressor of interest is increased from

Table 3.8 Determinants of immigration policy preferences: Testing the Heckscher-Ohlin and factor-proportions-analysis models

Variable	1992 Model 1	1992 Model 2	1994 Model 1	1994 Model 2	1996 Model 1	1996 Model 2
Occupation Wage	−0.349 (0.130)		−0.811 (0.135)		−0.541 (0.133)	
Education Years		−0.044 (0.010)		−0.074 (0.011)		−0.059 (0.012)
Gender	−0.022 (0.048)	−0.008 (0.046)	0.022 (0.056)	0.083 (0.054)	−0.020 (0.060)	0.024 (0.057)
Age	−0.000 (0.001)	−0.002 (0.001)	0.000 (0.002)	−0.002 (0.002)	0.004 (0.002)	0.002 (0.002)
Race	−0.207 (0.080)	−0.225 (0.080)	−0.222 (0.091)	−0.211 (0.092)	−0.238 (0.096)	−0.241 (0.097)
Hispanic	−0.064 (0.111)	−0.122 (0.110)	−0.306 (0.136)	−0.360 (0.137)	−0.124 (0.120)	−0.172 (0.121)
Immigrant	−0.158 (0.066)	−0.150 (0.066)	−0.213 (0.076)	−0.193 (0.076)	−0.220 (0.087)	−0.207 (0.087)
Party Identification	0.003 (0.013)	0.008 (0.013)	−0.006 (0.016)	−0.002 (0.016)	−0.023 (0.016)	−0.016 (0.016)
Ideology	0.057 (0.020)	0.050 (0.020)	0.054 (0.028)	0.041 (0.029)	0.080 (0.025)	0.072 (0.025)
Observations	2,485	2,485	1,795	1,795	1,714	1,714

Note: These results are multiple imputation estimates of ordered-probit coefficients based on the 10 imputed data sets for each year. Each cell reports the coefficient estimate and (in parentheses) its standard error. In both models the dependent variable is individual opinions about whether US policy should increase, decrease, or keep the same the annual number of legal immigrants. This variable is defined such that higher (lower) values indicate more restrictive (less restrictive) policy preferences. For brevity, estimated cut points are not reported.

one standard deviation below its sample mean to one standard deviation above while all other regressors are held constant at their means.

Table 3.9 reports results of these simulations for our two skills regressors. For 1992, increasing *Occupation Wage* from one standard deviation below its sample mean to one standard deviation above ($325 per week to $699 per week), with all other regressors held constant at their means, reduces the probability of supporting immigration restrictions by 0.049 on average. The 1992 results for *Education Years* are similar. Increasing

Table 3.9 Estimated effect of increasing skill levels on the probability of supporting immigration restrictions

Skills measure	1992	1994	1996
Occupation Wage	−0.049 (0.021) [−0.083, −0.013]	−0.135 (0.022) [−0.171, −0.100]	−0.095 (0.023) [−0.133, −0.057]
Education Years	−0.102 (0.020) [−0.133, −0.069]	−0.141 (0.022) [−0.175, −0.105]	−0.121 (0.025) [−0.162, −0.082]

Note: Using the estimates from models 1 and 2, we simulated the consequences of changing each skill measure from one standard deviation below its mean to one standard deviation above on the probability of supporting immigration restrictions. The mean effect is reported first, with the standard error of this estimate in parentheses followed by the 90 percent confidence interval.

Education Years by two standard deviations (about 10.1 years to 15.7 years), with all other regressors held constant at their means, reduces the probability of supporting immigration restrictions by 0.102 on average. The magnitude of these estimated effects was even larger for 1994 and 1996. The same result obtains for all three years of table 3.9: higher skill levels are strongly and significantly correlated with lower probabilities of supporting immigration restrictions. In words, this table indicates that if you could put a high school dropout with roughly 11 years of education through both high school and college, ending up with about 16 years of education, then the probability that this individual supports immigration restrictions would fall by some 10 to 14 percentage points.

Empirical Results: Does Local Immigrant Concentration Affect Immigration Policy Preferences?

The result that skill levels are correlated with immigration policy preferences is consistent both with the factor-proportions-analysis model and with an HO model in which immigration affects both wages and output mix. By pooling all regions together, however, we have not yet tested the area-analysis model. To do this, we modified our initial specifications by adding the regressor *High-Immigration MSA* and its interaction with skill levels. If preferences are consistent with the area-analysis model, then the correlation between skill levels and preferences should be stronger in gateway communities. Thus, we would expect a positive coefficient on *High-Immigration MSA* and a negative coefficient on its interaction with skill levels.

Table 3.10 presents the results for this specification, where model 3 uses *Occupation Wage* and model 4 uses *Education Years*. The results for all the nonskills regressors are qualitatively the same as before. Our skills measures are still negatively correlated with preferences at the 95 percent confidence level or better. But in neither case is *High-Immigration MSA* significantly positive or its interaction with skill levels significantly negative. Overall, the correlation between skill levels and immigration policy preferences is not higher among people in high-immigration areas than among people elsewhere. This finding is inconsistent with the area-analysis model.[14]

Robustness Checks for Immigration Policy Preferences

Again, a first check is to ask whether our results are robust to the inclusion of other regressors in the analysis. We have already demonstrated that the skills-preferences link holds even when the analysis controls for a standard set of demographic identifiers and measures of political orientation.[15] We also checked the robustness of our results by including a number of other regressors that might reasonably be expected to influence immigration opinions. Our main findings on skill levels and geography were consistently robust to our alternative specifications.

We also added a measure of the skill mix of immigrants in the local community. Recall that the NES surveys' immigration-policy preferences question does not specify any skill level of prospective immigrants, and that we have assumed that respondents think US immigrant inflows increase the relative supply of less-skilled workers. Different communities, however, may have very different skill mixes of immigrants, and thus how local citizens think about immigration policy may vary.

To try to control for this possibility, we obtained data on the educational attainment of the immigrant population in local communities as reported in the 1990 US census. We then defined the skill mix of immigrants by using three different educational cutoffs: the share with a high school degree or higher, the share with more than a high school degree, and the share with a college degree or higher. Adding this immigrant-skill-mix regressor to models 3 and 4 does not alter our results for local-labor-market effects. As for this new regressor itself, individuals living in communities

---

14. We also tested this specification using five other definitions of *High-Immigration MSA*. In almost every case the interaction term's coefficient was positive but not significant; in no case did the interaction term have a significantly negative coefficient or *High-Immigration MSA* a significantly positive one.

15. The correlation between skill levels and immigration opinions does not depend on these conditioning variables and holds in bivariate ordered-probit models.

Table 3.10 Determinants of immigration policy preferences: Testing the area-analysis model

Variable	1992 Model 3	1992 Model 4	1994 Model 3	1994 Model 4	1996 Model 3	1996 Model 4
Occupation Wage	−0.334 (0.161)		−0.801 (0.151)		−0.572 (0.150)	
Occupation Wage × High-Immigration MSA	−0.030 (0.309)		0.119 (0.291)		0.231 (0.319)	
Education Years		−0.054 (0.011)		−0.074 (0.013)		−0.061 (0.013)
Education Years × High-Immigration MSA		0.038 (0.019)		0.012 (0.024)		0.016 (0.030)
High-Immigration MSA	−0.005 (0.168)	−0.501 (0.264)	−0.218 (0.192)	−0.299 (0.343)	−0.206 (0.225)	−0.264 (0.441)
Gender	−0.021 (0.048)	−0.009 (0.046)	0.023 (0.056)	0.081 (0.054)	−0.022 (0.060)	0.023 (0.057)
Age	−0.000 (0.001)	−0.002 (0.001)	0.000 (0.002)	−0.002 (0.002)	0.004 (0.002)	0.002 (0.002)
Race	−0.204 (0.080)	−0.224 (0.078)	−0.206 (0.091)	−0.196 (0.092)	−0.231 (0.097)	−0.236 (0.098)
Hispanic	−0.057 (0.117)	−0.085 (0.115)	−0.250 (0.138)	−0.299 (0.138)	−0.102 (0.121)	−0.150 (0.125)
Immigrant	−0.154 (0.069)	−0.151 (0.069)	−0.176 (0.079)	−0.158 (0.079)	−0.206 (0.090)	−0.198 (0.090)
Party Identification	0.003 (0.013)	0.009 (0.013)	−0.007 (0.016)	−0.003 (0.017)	−0.023 (0.016)	−0.015 (0.016)
Ideology	0.057 (0.020)	0.050 (0.020)	0.052 (0.029)	0.040 (0.029)	0.079 (0.025)	0.072 (0.025)
Observations	2,485	2,485	1,795	1,795	1,714	1,714

MSA = metropolitan statistical area.

Note: These results are multiple imputation estimates of ordered-probit coefficients based on the 10 imputed data sets for each year. Each cell reports the coefficient estimate and (in parentheses) its standard error. In both models the dependent variable is individual opinions about whether US policy should increase, decrease, or keep the same the annual number of legal immigrants. This variable is defined such that higher (lower) values indicate more restrictive (less restrictive) policy preferences. For brevity, estimated cut points are not reported.

whose immigrant population has a higher skill mix are somewhat more likely to support more immigration: the estimated coefficients in models 3 and 4 are negative, significantly so in a minority of cases.[16]

Another consideration for evaluating our findings is whether the skills-preferences correlation for immigration could reflect some consideration other than labor-market pressures. In their analysis of immigration preferences, Citrin et al. (1997) assume that educational attainment does not measure labor-market skills. For example, education might indicate tolerance or civic awareness.

Further analysis, however, supports the interpretation of the skills-preferences correlation as labor-market pressures. One consideration that supports our interpretation is that results are qualitatively different when the full sample each year is split between those in and out of the labor force (with "in" defined either as employed or as unemployed but actively seeking work). If labor-market pressures drive the skills-preferences correlation, then it may be weaker among groups with weaker labor force attachment—that is, those out of the labor force relative to those in it. Most alternative hypotheses about what our skills variables measure would not predict a difference across these two groups of respondents.[17] In fact, we did find such a difference. There is a strong skills-preferences correlation for the working-only subsample, but a much weaker correlation—not

---

16. We thank George Borjas for providing us with these data. One might worry that each NES survey respondent interprets the immigration question to mean immigrants of the same skill level as the respondent him- or herself. Were this the case, one might reasonably expect every respondent to support more restrictive immigration policies. The fact that reported preferences look very different from this, and that we find a robust skills-preferences correlation, suggests that respondents are not interpreting the immigration question this way.

Another added regressor was union membership: union members preferred more restrictive immigration policy, an effect that was statistically significant in some specifications. Two other regressors were retrospective evaluations of the national economy and retrospective evaluations of personal finances. Both retrospective measures tended to have the expected sign—those with gloomier retrospections preferred more restrictive immigration policy—but were never statistically significant. We included state unemployment rates, another geography-varying regressor, to control in the cross-section for any business-cycle effect on immigration policy preferences. This regressor was never statistically significant, however. Finally, we included homeownership, which also was almost never statistically significant. Inclusion of these variables did not substantially affect our reported results for the link between skill levels and immigration opinions.

17. To the extent that most individuals out of the labor market truly are potential entrants who are aware of their labor-market options, a failure to detect a difference between the two subsamples does not imply a rejection of our skills interpretation of the results. So this test leads to a clear inference only if a difference is detected. Note that a similar analysis of the subsamples for trade opinions detected only slight and statistically insignificant differences in the impact of skill levels on opinions for respondents in and out of the labor force.

significantly different from zero in 1992 and 1996—for the not-in-labor-force subsample.[18]

As a second check on the interpretation of our skills regressors, we added to models 1 and 2 direct measures of ethnic and racial tolerance, as proxied by respondents' answers to three different tolerance statements or questions (e.g., "We should be more tolerant of people who choose to live according to their own moral standards, even if they are very different from our own"). In all specifications greater tolerance was significantly correlated with preferences for less restrictive immigration policy, but our significant skills-preferences correlation persisted. Overall, we interpret these two checks as evidence that *Occupation Wage* and *Education Years* measure labor-market skills.[19]

Summary

Preferences about trade and immigration policy divide strongly across skill levels. Less-skilled individuals, measured in standard labor-economics terms such as educational attainment or average wage, are much more likely to oppose freer trade and immigration than their more-skilled counterparts. No strong evidence emerged in our analyses for many other commonly supposed cleavages. For trade, industry of employment is not systematically related to trade policy preferences. Those working in "trade-exposed" industries, such as textiles and apparel, are not more likely to oppose freer trade, once we control for their skill levels. For immigration, people living in immigration gateway communities are not more or less likely to oppose freer immigration.[20]

---

18. The reported occupation for those not in the labor force is their most recent job. Also, we obtained the same results qualitatively from an alternative specification of our skills test in which we pooled the full sample and interacted skill levels with a dichotomous variable for labor force status participation. The split-sample test is more general, as it does not constrain the nonskills regressors to have the same coefficient for both labor force groups.

19. We also tried other measures of our skills and immigration regressors. For skills we tried dichotomous variables of educational attainment (high school dropouts, high school graduates, some college, and college and beyond) to look for any nonlinearities in how skill levels affect preferences. We discovered no clear nonlinearities: the relative coefficients on the dichotomous measures seemed consistent with an overall linear effect. We also tried respondents' previous-year income, and obtained qualitatively similar results to those for *Occupation Wage* and *Education Years*. In addition to the six measures of *High-Immigration MSA* discussed earlier, we also tried a dichotomous measure of residence in one of the "big six" immigrant states—California, Florida, Illinois, New Jersey, New York, and Texas. We also tried measuring immigration concentration with a continuous variable (the foreign-born share of each area's population) or with *High-Immigration MSA* plus an analogous low-immigration dummy variable. With all these measures we found no evidence of preferences consistent with the area-analysis model.

20. For corroborating evidence on the skills-preferences cleavage from other public opinion surveys, see appendix D.

This finding leads naturally to the question of what sorts of labor-market pressures have been facing different skill groups in the US economy and what role globalization may have played in these pressures. That is the subject of the next chapter.

4

Labor-Market Pressures Facing Workers

Chapter 2 documented the breadth and depth of antiglobalization sentiment among US citizens. Chapter 3 showed that preferences about trade and immigration policy divide strongly across skill levels. How is this evidence on worker perceptions and preferences related to worker pressures in the US economy? To answer this question, we first need to present evidence on these pressures. In this chapter we present this evidence, and in chapter 5 we return to the question of the relationship between worker perceptions, preferences, and pressures.

At the time of this writing, many macroeconomic measures of the US economy suggested healthy times for all US workers. US GDP had been expanding uninterrupted for a decade (nearly two decades but for the 1990-91 recession), the longest peacetime expansion in US history. Aggregate US unemployment had reached near-record lows in recent years, moving below 5 percent after 1997 and at times below 4 percent. Reflecting this ongoing economic growth, US financial wealth had grown tremendously: the New York Stock Exchange index rose nearly tenfold, from 71.11 at year-end 1981 to 650.30 at year-end 1999.[1]

Many commentators have puzzled over the juxtaposition of strong skepticism about globalization in the face of strong macroeconomic performance. As Gerald F. Seib put it in the *Wall Street Journal*, "After eight years of economic growth, obviously enhanced by international trade, at a time of the lowest unemployment rate in 30 years, a large chunk of Americans remain oddly ambivalent about the benefits of trade. One can

---

1. Equities data were obtained from the New York Stock Exchange, http://www.nyse.com/pdfs/historical99.pdf.

only wonder: What will their attitude be when economic times aren't so good?" (*Wall Street Journal*, 10 May 2000, A28).

What the macroeconomic performance misses, however, is the very different labor-market performance of different skill groups evident at the microeconomic level in recent decades. Indeed, the skills-preferences opinion cleavage described in chapter 3 suggests that economic performance across different skill groups is what matters. If different skill groups have fared differently, then one could conjecture a link between this differential economic performance and the skills-preference cleavage. To better understand links between worker perceptions, preferences, and pressures, in this chapter we present empirical evidence on the labor-market pressures facing different US skill groups in recent decades.

Wage trends across skill groups have differed dramatically in recent decades. First, the premium that more-skilled workers have earned over less-skilled workers has been rising sharply since the late 1970s. Second, average real-wage growth in the United States has been sluggish since the early 1970s. All this means that compared with high-skilled workers, the majority of the US labor force has had close to zero or even negative real-wage growth for about 25 years. During this period, only more-skilled workers have been enjoying real-wage gains. These patterns differ sharply from those of earlier decades, when real-wage growth was both faster and enjoyed by all groups, with steady or declining inequality.

What role has globalization played in driving these wage changes? On balance, most academic research has concluded that trade, immigration, and foreign direct investment have had relatively small roles. The real-wage slowdown remains largely a puzzle, but it has been most pronounced in the service sector, much of which is nontraded and has little FDI activity. Technological change favoring skilled workers seems to have been the major force driving up the returns to skills. There is little evidence that increases in trade, FDI, or immigration played the main role in widening inequality—although this is not to say globalization has had no role at all.

Thus, the data indicate poor labor-market performance for less-skilled US workers, in both relative and real terms, whereas the academic research suggests that globalization has not been the central force driving this performance. How these labor-market pressures are related to worker perceptions and preferences is the topic of chapter 5.

Changes in US Relative and Real Wages

Fact 1: Rising Inequality across Skills

Figure 4.1 shows one approximate measure of the rising US skills premium.[2] For each year since 1958, the figure plots the average annual

---

2. As discussed in chapter 3, economists typically distinguish different skill groups in terms of educational attainment, job classification, or work experience. Different measures have

Figure 4.1 The skill premium in US manufacturing

relative wage,
nonproduction to production workers

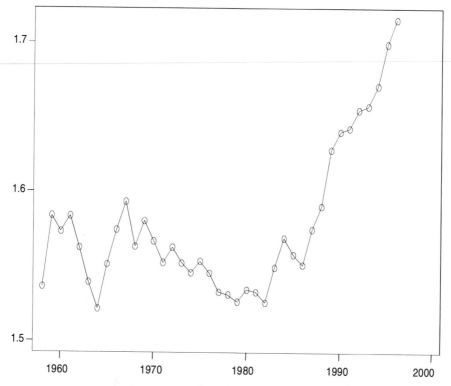

Note: Skill premium is measured as the ratio of average annual wages of nonproduction workers to average annual wages of production workers in US manufacturing.

Source: National Bureau of Economic Research, Manufacturing Industry Database, http://www.nber.org/nberces.

earnings of a nonproduction worker divided by the average annual earnings of a production worker in US manufacturing, where research has shown that nonproduction workers tend to have more labor-market skills than production workers. This ratio of nonproduction to production earnings, one possible measure of the skills premium, generally declined from the late 1950s until the late 1970s. But since about 1979 it has been rising sharply. In 1979 the average nonproduction worker earned about 50 percent more than the average production worker; by 1996 this gap had grown to over 70 percent.

different pros and cons, but it is important to stress that major labor-market shifts—such as the rising US skill premium—tend to look very similar across all measures.

This rise in the US skills premium has been under way since the late 1970s across all skills measures—education, experience, and job classification. For example, in 1979 male college-educated workers earned 30 percent more on average than male high school-educated workers. By 1995 this premium for college-educated workers had risen to about 70 percent. A similar picture of rising inequality can be found in the overall wage distribution. Both the 90/50 and the 50/10 earnings ratios for male workers—that is, the ratio of the earnings of a worker at the 90th percentile to those of a worker with median earnings and the ratio of a worker with median earnings to those of a worker at the 10th percentile—were flat or declining from 1967 until about 1979 and then rose steadily from 1979 through 1995. The exact timing and magnitude of the skills-premium changes vary somewhat with the data series used, but all series show the same dramatic picture of sharply rising returns to skills.[3]

Fact 2: Sluggish Growth in Average Real Wages

Along with these relative-wage changes, average real-wage growth in the United States has been sluggish since the early 1970s. Figure 4.2 illustrates this real-wage slowdown. For all nonfarm workers in the private sector each year since 1964, the figure plots US average weekly earnings in real 1982 dollars (nominal dollars deflated by a price index set equal to one in 1982). From 1964 through 1973, US average real weekly earnings rose strongly, from just over $280 to nearly $320. But since 1973 real earnings have slid dramatically, falling below $260 by the mid 1990s. By 2000, real earnings had recovered to just under $280, back to early-1980s levels but still well below the 1973 peak.

Of course, the exact pattern of change in US real wages depends on both the measure of nominal wages (e.g., just salary or all compensation including fringes) and the measure of the price index used to translate nominal into real wages (e.g., a consumer price index or a producer price index). A good deal of research has examined these measurement issues (e.g., the 1997 *Economic Report of the President* and Abraham, Spletzer, and Stewart 1999). But across a wide range of possible real-wage measures, a consistent pattern is seen: growth in average real earnings in the United States has been sluggish since the early 1970s.

Facts 1 and 2 Combined: Sluggish to Negative Real-Wage Growth for Most US Workers

The combination of the sharp rise in income inequality with the sharp slowdown in real-wage growth means that real-wage growth has been

---

3. These basic facts on relative earnings come from the *Economic Report of the President* for 1997 and for 2000, each of which devotes substantial space to labor markets and inequality.

Figure 4.2 Private-sector nonfarm average weekly earnings

1982 dollars

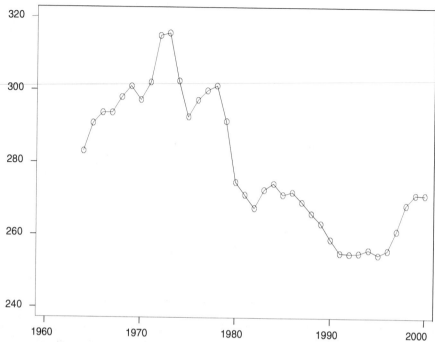

Note: Average real earnings are measured as weekly earnings expressed in seasonally adjusted 1982 dollars (price deflator is the consumer price index for urban wage earners and clerical workers—CPI-W). Each year's earnings are calculated by taking a simple arithmetic average of that year's 12 monthly earnings, except for 2000, where the average is taken over the 10 months through October.

Source: US Department of Labor, Bureau of Labor Statistics, Nonfarm Payroll Statistics from the Current Employment Statistics, Total Private Average Weekly Earnings, 1982 Dollars, Seasonally Adjusted (data series EES00500051), http://www.bls.gov/datahome.htm.

flat or even negative for less-skilled US workers in recent decades. Figure 4.3 shows this trend. Real-wage patterns are plotted from 1973 to 1998 for four different skill groups: more-skilled workers at the 90th percentile of the overall wage distribution; medium-skilled workers at the 50th percentile; less-skilled workers at the 10th percentile; and workers earning the statutory minimum wage. For each group, wages are benchmarked to 1979 levels, so the four lines intersect at zero that year. Only more-skilled workers at the 90th percentile enjoyed higher real wages in 1998

Inequality has risen across education, experience, and occupational groups as well as within these groups. For additional discussion, see Blanchflower and Slaughter (1999).

Figure 4.3 Differential real-wage performance across skill groups

real growth relative to 1979

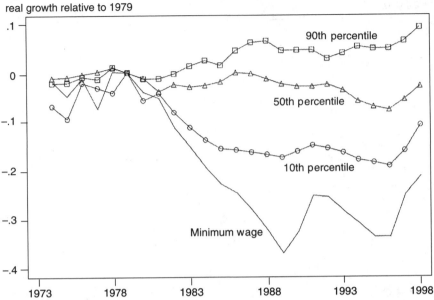

Note: Average real earnings are measured as nominal earnings deflated by the CPI-UX1 consumer price index. Wage growth for four different skill groups is shown: more-skilled workers at the 90th percentile of the overall wage distribution; medium-skilled workers at the 50th percentile; less-skilled workers at the 10th percentile; and workers earning the statutory minimum wage. Each group's real-wage growth is plotted relative to its 1979 level, which is set equal to 0.

Source: Katz and Krueger (1999, figure 4).

than in 1979; real wages for all other skill groups were lower in 1998 than 1979.

Again, exact real-wage movements depend on many measurement issues, but the overall pattern of different real-wage performance across skill groupings is clear for all measures. Similarly, the 2000 *Economic Report of the President* describes the dramatically different real-income performance for families across different quintiles of the overall income distribution. From 1973 to 1993, the bottom 40 percent of families suffered real-income declines—nearly 1 percent per year for those in the lowest quintile, and about 0.3 percent per year for those in the second quintile. Those in the third quintile had basically zero real-income growth. Only families in the fourth and fifth quintiles enjoyed real-income increases, about 0.4 percent and 1.3 percent per year, respectively. Thus, from 1973 through 1993, 60 percent of US households had flat or declining real income. Looking at less-skilled groups, Freeman (1995) reports that the real hourly earnings of male high school graduates fell by 20 percent from

Table 4.1 The skill mix of the US labor force since 1940 (percent)

Year	High school dropouts	High school graduates	Some college	College graduates
1940	76	14	5	5
1950	66	21	7	6
1963	52	30	9	9
1970	45	34	10	11
1979	32	37	15	16
1989	23	39	17	21
1999	17	33	25	25

Note: Each cell reports the share of the total US adult population (aged 25 and over) accounted for by that labor group in that year.

Sources: Johnson (1997, table 1) for all years but 1999. For 1999: US Bureau of Census (2000), *Educational Attainment in the United States, March 1999*, Washington: US Government Printing Office.

1979 through 1993, with an even larger 30 percent decline for "entry-level" male high school graduates.

How big a part of the US labor force are these less-skilled workers who have suffered poor wage performance, both in real and relative terms, for some 25 years now? As typically defined by labor economists, they constitute the majority of the US labor force. Table 4.1 shows the skill mix among US workers since 1940. The US labor force has been upgrading skills for decades. In absolute terms, however, even as of 1999, college graduates—the group typically defined as the most-skilled workers— accounted for only about one in four US workers. Adding those with some college still captures only 50 percent. Even after 60 years of rising educational attainment, the median US worker is still a high-school graduate and has seen poor wage performance in both real and relative terms for more than a generation.

We make two final points about US wages. First, real-wage growth for all skill groups has been much stronger since about 1996, but the impressive gains of the past few years have not undone the poor performance of the past few decades. Figures 4.2 and 4.3 illustrate this strength for all workers and for different skill groups. The same strength is evident in other earnings data. For example, the 2000 *Economic Report of the President* reports real-income growth of 2 to 2.5 percent across all five family income quintiles from 1993 to 1998. This real-wage growth at all parts of the skills distribution is important, and research findings are beginning to emerge on whether advances in computers and information technology have driven this growth (e.g., the symposium in the Fall 2000 *Journal of Economic Perspectives*). Placing this recent growth in context, however, shows that it has not offset the flat or negative growth of recent decades. Figure 4.2 shows that average real earnings in 2000 returned to early-1980s levels—which were still well below pre-1980 levels. Similarly, figure 4.3 shows that the growth of 1996-98 did not return wages to 1979 levels for workers at the 50th and 10th percentiles.

The second point to note is that recent US wage changes differ markedly from US wage movements earlier in the 20th century. Krugman (1992) reports that from 1900 to 1970, US output per worker rose at an average annual rate of 2.3 percent, reaching the rate of 2.8 percent during the 1950s and 1960s. From 1970 through the start of the 1990s, output per worker grew at only 1.2 percent per year. To the extent that workers earn their marginal product, these productivity measures also indicate the likely pattern of real wages.[4] In earlier decades, inequality across skill levels and households was generally flat or falling. For example, from 1948 through 1973, family income grew faster for the lowest quintile than for the highest (*Economic Report of the President* 2000).

Has Globalization Driven Recent US Wage Changes?

The globalization of the US economy depicted earlier in figures 1.1 through 1.3 suggests that the answer might be yes. Each figure shows sizeable increases in globalization over roughly the same period that labor-market performance deteriorated. However, the answer is not as clear as that, because most academic research has concluded that increased trade, immigration, and foreign direct investment have *not* been the most important forces driving shifts in real and relative wages.

Consider real wages first. As noted earlier, the real-wage slowdown has been most pronounced in services, which are largely nontraded and have little FDI activity. From 1973 through 1993, real output per hour in US manufacturing grew at an average annual rate of about 2.5 percent. But in the nonfarm private sector, real output per hour grew at an average annual rate of only 1.4 percent. Thus, the productivity slowdown was concentrated mainly outside of US manufacturing and agriculture—that is, in the part of the economy that is mainly nontradable and in which

---

4. Although in theory there should be a virtually one-to-one relationship between productivity or output per worker and real wages, in practice there can be differences. For example, the 2000 *Economic Report of the President* reports that US real output per hour grew annually at 3.3 percent from 1948 through 1973, but at only 1.5 percent from 1973 through 1990, with even slower growth in real compensation, 0.8 percent per year, from 1973 to 1993.

production is much less related to FDI.[5] Many researchers have used evidence like this to cast doubt on arguments that the US real-wage slowdown has been driven by globalization forces.

What about the rising US skills premium? The academic literature on this subject is extensive, and it offers a wide range of conclusions (see surveys in Freeman 1995 and Richardson 1995). However, most studies seem to have concluded that technological change favoring skilled workers has been the major force driving up returns to skills. This "skill-biased" technological change, widespread across the majority of US industries, does not appear to be robustly related to various globalization forces. Consider each force in turn.

Most trade economists looking at the role of international trade have organized their data analyses around the Stolper-Samuelson process outlined in chapter 3. For trade to have driven changes in US relative wages via changes in US relative product prices, it would have done so by raising the relative price of less-skill-intensive goods during the 1970s but then lowering the relative price of less-skill-intensive goods since around 1980. Have prices actually moved in this manner? No: changes in US product prices have not clearly matched up with changes in the skills premium. This has led many to conclude that trade has not been a major force driving wage movements. Other studies using other methods have reached similar conclusions.[6]

The literature examining the impact of immigration on native wages in US regions is also extensive. The standard approach is to regress the change in native wages on the change in the stock of immigrants across US metropolitan areas. Most studies find that immigration has, at most, a small negative impact on local native wages. As for FDI, there is no robust correlation between either outward or inward flows.[7]

This is not to say that trade, immigration, and FDI have had *no* role in *any* recent US wage changes. A number of studies have concluded that these globalization forces have played some part. For example, Feenstra

---

5. These productivity data come from the Bureau of Labor Statistics, http://146.142.4.24/cgi-bin/surveymost?pr.

6. Leamer (1998) and Baldwin and Cain (2000) find that US relative product prices fell for less-skill-intensive sectors during the 1970s. And these two studies as well as Lawrence and Slaughter (1993) and Bhagwati (1991) find no clear trend in US relative product prices during the 1980s. See Slaughter (2000a) for a survey of these product-price studies. Borjas et al. (1997) calculate trade's role in rising inequality by calculating changes in US labor supplies "embodied" in flows of US exports and imports. This is a very different methodology from the product-price studies, but they also find only a small role for trade.

7. Recent immigration papers include Borjas et al. (1997) and Card (1997). See Borjas (1994 and 1999) and Friedberg and Hunt (1995) for surveys. See Slaughter (2000b) and Blonigen and Slaughter (2000) for studies of outward and inward FDI and skill upgrading within US industries.

and Hanson (1999) find strong evidence that "outsourcing"—that is, importing intermediate inputs—in US manufacturing accounts for about 15 percent of the overall rise from 1979 to 1990 in the manufacturing skills premium. In contrast, their proxy for technological change, computer use, accounts for about 35 percent of the overall rise—more than twice as much. And despite the ambiguous product-price evidence, Leamer (1998) argues that greater international trade has played a role. Borjas et al. (1997) argue that immigration's wage effects should appear nationally rather than in local labor markets and conclude that greater immigrant inflows have helped pressure the wages of high school dropouts.

The appropriate measurement of these globalization pressures has been the subject of a great deal of sharp methodological debate—and, not surprisingly, different methods have led to different conclusions. However, most academic researchers have concluded that technological change, not globalization, has been the major force affecting US labor markets in recent decades. In a recent survey of many prominent economists about the relative contribution of various forces to the rising US skills premium, the average of their responses was that technological change has accounted for 45 percent of the rise, trade about 10 percent, and immigration only about 5 percent (*Economic Report of the President* 1997, 175).

Summary

In this chapter we have shown that compared with high-skilled workers, the majority of the US labor force has experienced poor relative and real-wage performance in recent decades. On balance, most academic research has found that technological change, not globalization, has been the major force affecting US labor markets in recent decades. Given this evidence on labor-market pressures facing US workers, we now turn to links between these pressures and worker perceptions.

5

Worker Perceptions and Pressures in the Global Economy

Is There a "Disconnect" between Worker Perceptions and Pressures in the United States?

We have presented evidence on both worker perceptions and pressures in an increasingly global US economy. As for perceptions about globalization, a wide range of public opinion surveys indicate that US citizens recognize both the costs and the benefits of integration with the world economy. But on balance, the public seems to weigh the costs more than the benefits, so that their perceptions are translated into generally skeptical policy preferences about the liberalization of trade, immigration, and foreign direct investment. Moreover, these preferences divide strongly across skill levels: less-educated, lower-income workers are much more likely to oppose policies aimed at freer trade and immigration. As for pressures in the US labor market, these workers, still the majority of the US labor force, have had close to zero or even negative real-wage growth for more than 25 years thanks to the combination of slow growth in average real wages and sharp rises in inequality of relative wages across skill groups.

How are these perceptions, policy preferences, and labor-market pressures related to each other? One hypothesis is that the labor-market pressures have produced the policy preferences. That is, amid poor real and relative-wage performance, less-skilled US workers have blamed globalization for these outcomes and thus have been more likely to oppose policies aimed at further liberalization.

We present two pieces of evidence to support this hypothesis. One is responses to a set of survey questions suggesting that public support for trade liberalization declined at roughly the same time as the downturn in US labor-market performance. The other is responses to a set of survey questions showing that a majority of Americans do think that globalization has hurt the US labor market.

First, consider time-series evidence on public support for trade liberalization. The data from chapter 4 show that the poor labor-market performance of US less-skilled workers began in the mid to late 1970s. Did public opinion about globalization change with the decline in labor-market performance? If it did, this association could be consistent with the hypothesis that labor-market pressures shape policy preferences (although, as we discuss below, it need not be if people are forward-looking regarding labor-market pressures). Ideally we would be able to test this association using data from a continuous time series of identically worded questions. We do not have this kind of data, but we are able to use two different kinds of similarly worded trade policy questions. Data from both sets of questions suggest a decline in public support for liberalization occurring at roughly the same time as the downturn in labor market outcomes.

One set of questions, asked in 1957 and 1983, is of the "is trade good or bad" variety.[1]

Question:	What about tariffs on foreign goods? Do you think tariffs should be fairly high to protect people's jobs and our own industry from foreign competition, or should they be fairly low to keep prices down and encourage international trade?
Responses:	High: 34% Low: 34% Medium (vol.): 10% Depends (vol.): 6% Don't know: 16%

Source: Roper, March 1957

Question:	Some people favor increasing taxes on foreign imports to protect American jobs in certain industries. Others oppose increasing import taxes because it would lead to higher consumer prices for certain products. Which comes closest to your opinion?
Responses:	Favor: 55% Oppose: 36% Don't know: 9%

Source: Gallup/*Newsweek*, May 1983

---

1. In these surveys, certain volunteered responses—that is, responses other than the choices presented by the interviewer—were recorded, coded, and tallied. These are identified with the abbreviation "vol." in the results.

In 1957, respondents were evenly divided on whether they thought tariffs should be high to protect jobs or low to keep prices down. In 1983, 55 percent of respondents favored higher tariffs to protect American jobs, and 36 percent were opposed. In similarly phrased questions asked in the late 1980s and 1990s (see chapter 2), a clear majority of respondents favored the more protectionist response, as in 1983.

The other set of questions, asked in five surveys conducted between 1945 and 1981, does not address trade's costs and benefits but instead asks about higher or lower tariffs in general.

Question:	Are you in favor of high tariffs or low tariffs for this country?
Responses:	High: 39% Low: 34% No opinion: 28%

Source: Gallup, September 1945

Question:	By and large, do you favor higher tariffs or lower tariffs than we have at present?
Answers, 1959:	Higher: 31% Lower: 40% Same (vol.): 18% No opinion: 11%
Answers, 1961:	Higher: 32% Lower: 40% Same (vol.): 14% No opinion: 14%

Source: Gallup, May 1959 and December 1961

Question:	Frequently on any controversial issue there is no clear-cut side that people take, and also frequently solutions on controversial issues are worked out by compromise. But I'm going to name some different things, and for each one would you tell me whether on balance you would be more in favor of it, or more opposed to it? . . . High tariffs on goods imported by the United States from other countries.
Responses:	Favor: 47% Oppose: 31% Have mixed feelings (vol.)/Don't know: 22%

Source: Roper, January 1978

Question: Frequently on any controversial issue there is no
                   clear-cut side that people take, and also fre-
                   quently solutions on controversial issues are
                   worked out by compromise. But I'm going to
                   name some different things, and for each one
                   would you tell me whether on balance you
                   would be more in favor of it, or more opposed
                   to it? . . . High tariffs on goods imported by the
                   United States from other countries.

Responses: Favor: 50%
                   Oppose: 28%
                   Have mixed feelings (vol.)/Don't know: 22%

Source: Roper, January 1981

These questions show a pattern similar to that of the first set: responses
before the 1970s appear less protectionist. Given the amount of data and
the lack of comparable questions, this time-series evidence is by no means
conclusive. However, it is broadly consistent with the hypothesis that
labor-market pressures have influenced US opinion about globalization.[2]

The second piece of evidence supporting this hypothesis is what individuals themselves have to say about the connection. Recall from chapter
2 that the large majority of Americans worry that international trade
generates labor-market costs in terms of job destruction and lower wages.
But when asked about these costs not in the abstract but rather with
direct reference to recent US wage developments, do Americans think
that globalization has mattered? The limited survey evidence on this
question suggests that the answer is yes.

Question: Do you agree or disagree with the following
                   statement: Most American trade agreements
                   with foreign countries are a principal cause of
                   lost jobs and a lower standard of living in this
                   country?

Responses: Agree: 63%
                   Disagree: 32%
                   Don't know: 5%

Source: CNN/*Time,* October 1995

Nearly two-thirds of Americans think that trade has been "a principal
cause" of lower US living standards. However, this question does not
ask for respondents' opinions about trade's role relative to other forces.
The next question does. What is striking is that for every respondent
citing technological change as the primary cause of slow real-wage growth

---

2. One point that should be clear, given our evaluation of the time-series evidence, is that
public opinion is *not* markedly more skeptical about globalization in the 1990s than in the
late 1970s and 1980s.

(9 percent of respondents), three groups of respondents cite globalization as the primary cause (30 percent total: 11 percent for immigration, 11 percent for foreign competition, and 8 percent for jobs going overseas).

Question: Many economic experts say that American wages are not rising as fast as they could, that is, wages are not keeping up with inflation and increases in the cost of living. To the extent that this is true, which of the following reasons would you say is most responsible for causing wages to rise slowly in the United States?

Responses: Corporate greed: 26%
Lack of education: 15%
Illegal immigrants: 11%
Foreign competition: 11%
New technology requiring fewer workers: 9%
Jobs going overseas: 8%
Competition at home: 5%
Undecided: 15%

Source: EPIC/MRA, April 1998

What about rising wage inequality? A large majority of Americans think that trade has contributed to this trend—five times as many as those who think that trade has worked against it.

Question: Do you think that the growth of international trade has increased the gap between rich and poor in this country, decreased the gap, or has had no effect?

Responses: Increased: 56.2%
Decreased: 10.4%
Neither: 27.2%
Don't know/refused: 6.1%

Source: Program on International Policy Attitudes, October 1999

The responses appear to cleave across skill groups for this question, with less-educated workers more likely to think that trade has been widening inequality.

Question: Do you think that the growth of international trade has increased the gap between rich and poor in this country, decreased the gap, or has had no effect?

"Increase" responses:
        Those with college degree or more: 50%
        Those with some college: 53%
        Those with high school degree: 55%
        Those with less than high school: 70%

Source: Program on International Policy Attitudes, October 1999

If one describes the redistribution lines generated by trade in terms of "business" versus "workers," Americans again seem to think that trade has worsened income distributions.

Question: As you may know, international trade has increased substantially in recent years. I would like to know how positive or negative you think the growth of international trade is, for certain groups of people. Please answer on a scale from 0 to 10, with 0 being completely negative, 10 being completely positive, and 5 being equally positive and negative.

Answers for "American business":
      Mean: 6.14
      Median: 7.00
      Percent over 5: 61%

Answers for "American workers":
      Mean: 4.53
      Median: 5.00
      Percent over 5: 25%

Source: Program on International Policy Attitudes, October 1999

Thus, the hypothesis that labor-market pressures have had a role in the formation of public perceptions and policy preferences is supported both by time-series evidence on declining support for trade liberalization and by direct questions about this linkage. It seems plausible that amid poor real and relative-wage performance, less-skilled US workers have blamed globalization for these outcomes and thus have been more likely to oppose policies aimed at further liberalization.

Chapter 4 showed, however, that most academic researchers have concluded that technological change, not globalization, has been the major force affecting US labor markets in recent decades. Is there somehow a "disconnect" between the academic research and this hypothesis linking labor-market pressures to policy perceptions? No, for at least three reasons.

First, the academic research does not uniformly conclude that globalization has had no effect on US wages, particularly the rise in wage inequality. Again, in the survey of prominent economists mentioned in chapter 4, the role of trade was estimated at 10 percent, compared with 45 percent for technology—but 10 percent is hardly negligible.

Second, in evaluating US policy, people may be forward-looking. Even if all US citizens thought that globalization has not affected US labor markets in the past, they may still think that globalization will affect them in the future. On the trade side, Haskel and Slaughter (2000) have shown that the US tariffs remaining at the end of the Tokyo Round of the General Agreement on Tariffs and Trade (GATT) were highest in the less-skill-intensive sectors—in particular, textiles, apparel, and footwear. This finding suggests that there may be scope for future trade liberalizations—in particular, the Multifiber Arrangement phase-outs under the GATT's Uruguay Round—to pressure US less-skilled wages. On the immigration side, Borjas (1999) has examined how US less-skilled wages are likely to be pressured further if current US immigration policy is not altered to increase the skill mix of arriving immigrants. Hence there is reason to suppose that future US liberalizations will pressure US less-skilled wages.

Third, people may simply think that technological change is a force unimpeded by government policy, and so may opt for protectionist trade, immigration, and FDI policies to address labor-market pressures. Suppose Americans generally held the same views as the polled economists, thinking that technological change has been many times more important than trade or immigration in widening US inequality. They may still opt for protection because they do not think that policy can slow the advance of technology. Recall from chapter 2 that 61 percent of Americans think that trade protection can halt trade's growth.[3]

Thus, in many ways, worker perceptions about globalization appear to be in accord with the worker pressures of globalization. Indeed, making this connection between worker interests and opinions is one of the key contributions of this study. Although concerns about the impact of globalization on the environment, human rights, and other issues are an important part of the politics of globalization, it is the connection between policy liberalization, worker interests, and individual opinions that forms the foundation for the US public's skepticism about liberalization.

This conclusion suggests many interesting questions that we leave open. For example, our evidence linking individuals' economic interests in policy options with their preferences about these options does not preclude political leaders and the media from influencing public opinion.[4] And our analysis has demonstrated how the globalization backlash resonates

---

3. The connection between preferences and pressures is further bolstered by the numerous analyses in chapter 3 that evaluated our interpretation of the empirical link between skills and preferences.

4. As we document in chapter 2, opinions about globalization are characterized by low information and uncertainty. Under such circumstances, "elite" debate may influence opinion formation. Although we do not think it likely that elites can lead opinions about globalization in any direction, under such circumstances it seems reasonable to believe that they can influence things like the connections the public makes between globalization and labor-market performance. Evaluation of the effects of elite debate on globalization opinions is an important topic for future research. With this caveat in mind, it is important to recall that our analysis of both the broad patterns and cleavages in public opinion about globalization includes data for which the distribution and intensity of elite debate varies. Consequently, we think our characterization of these *central tendencies* of public opinion on globalization are robust to these further considerations (e.g., see our analysis of the effects of political awareness in chapter 3).

with widely held public opinion that divides strongly across skill groups. As the policy actions of this backlash are the outcome of interactions among policy preferences, collective-action problems, and political institutions, we have added one piece to the puzzle of understanding the backlash.

Policy Implications

What do our findings have to say to policymakers? In closing, we offer two policy implications suggested by our analysis.

First is simply the need to acknowledge the skills-preferences opinion cleavage and the breadth of antiglobalization sentiments it implies in the United States today. In chapter 1 we cited recent antiglobalization events such as the November 1999 WTO protests in Seattle. However, much of the media coverage on that and other such events has left unclear whether those protesting were simply unrepresentative fringe groups or whether their concerns resonate with attitudes among the broader American public. The latter is closer to the truth. It is not just vandalizing "anarchists" in Seattle or just union workers from selected trade-affected industries who oppose globalization policies. It is a much broader share of US citizens, dividing strongly across skill groups. This finding is consistent with the idea that globalization's labor-market pressures affect certain skill groups across all industries thanks to domestic labor-market competition.

Second, the skills-preferences cleavage suggests that US support for liberalization will be broader if adjustment assistance is targeted to individuals in particular skill groups. Survey evidence indicates that Americans are more likely to support liberalization when it is explicitly linked with assistance aimed at minimizing labor-market costs. First, a majority of Americans regard current trade assistance to be inadequate.

Question:	I would like to know your impression of government efforts to help retrain workers who have lost jobs due to international trade. Do you think those efforts have been . . .
Responses:	More than adequate: 2.2% Adequate: 29.1% Not adequate: 56.9% Don't know/refused: 11.8%

Source: Program on International Policy Attitudes, October 1999

And when asked what constituencies current US trade policy favors, large majorities of Americans think that too little attention is paid to average Americans or working Americans, with a commensurate majority who think that too much attention is paid to "multinational corporations." This finding is consistent with the idea that citizens want policy to focus not just on liberalization but also on its effect on US workers.

Question: I would like to know your sense about the US
                 government officials who are making decisions
                 about US international trade policy. How much
                 do you think they consider concerns [of the fol-
                 lowing groups]?

Answers for "general American public":
                 Too much: 5.3%
                 Too little: 68.3%
                 About right: 24.6%
                 Don't know/refused: 1.8%

Answers for "working Americans":
                 Too much: 2.2%
                 Too little: 72.4%
                 About right: 23.3%
                 Don't know/refused: 2.1%

Answers for "multinational corporations":
                 Too much: 54.2%
                 Too little: 14.5%
                 About right: 24.2%
                 Don't know/refused: 7.1%

Source: Program on International Policy Attitudes, October 1999

Support for trade liberalization is higher when, rather than being por-
trayed as a yes-or-no option, a third alternative is offered—to liberalize
slowly to allow more time for worker adjustment.

Question: As you may know, international trade has
                 increased substantially in recent years. This
                 increase is largely due to the lowering of trade
                 barriers between countries by, for example, lower-
                 ing import taxes. Lowering trade barriers is a con-
                 troversial issue. Here are three positions on the
                 issue. Which comes closest to your point of view?
                 A: We should keep up barriers against interna-
                 tional trade, because importing cheap products
                 from other countries threatens American jobs.
                 B: We should remove trade barriers now because
                 this allows Americans to sell in other countries
                 what they do the best job of producing, and to
                 buy products that other countries do the best job
                 producing, saving everybody money.
                 C: We should lower trade barriers, but only gradu-
                 ally, so American workers can have time to adjust
                 to the changes that come with international trade.

Responses: Statement A: 31.3%
                 Statement B: 24.0%
                 Statement C: 42.9%
                 Don't know/refused: 1.8%

Source: Program on International Policy Attitudes, October 1999

In consonance with the evidence from chapter 2, the share of protectionist preferences is larger than the share of liberalizing preferences. However, a plurality of respondents select the third option, to liberalize slowly to facilitate adjustment. Even more dramatic is that when a policy option makes explicit the need for liberalization to be linked with government adjustment policies, fully two-thirds of respondents select it.

Question: As you may know, there are various views on the question of whether the US should promote freer trade. There are also different views on the question of whether the US government should have programs that try to help workers who lose their jobs because of free trade. Which of the following three positions comes closest to your point of view?

A: I favor free trade, and I believe that it IS necessary for the government to have programs to help workers who lose their jobs.

B: I favor free trade, and I believe that it is NOT necessary for the government to have programs to help workers who lose their jobs.

C: I do not favor free trade.

Responses: Statement A: 66.3%
Statement B: 17.6%
Statement C: 14.3%
Don't know/refused: 1.9%

Source: Program on International Policy Attitudes, October 1999

Our evidence on the skills-preferences correlation suggests that adjustment policies will have maximal effect when targeted by skills. It is the less-educated, lower-income US workers who tend to be most concerned about globalization, regardless of industry of employment; hence it is to this group that adjustment policies should be directed. Adjustment policies targeted at particular industries may be inadequately narrow. For example, eligibility for the Trade Adjustment Assistance (TAA) program hinges on job dislocations from a set of industries administratively determined to be affected by trade. Our analysis suggests that this industry focus misses the large majority of those concerned about trade liberalization, because the majority of US workers are employed in nontraded industries.[5] Today in the United States, calls for policies to "improve US skills" are widespread. Our analysis suggests a novel motivation for such policies: to better address concerns about globalization.

---

5. In the United States today, more people work either in retail trade or in government at all levels than in all of manufacturing.

APPENDICES

Appendix A
The Theory of Policy Cleavages

This appendix expands on the section "Theory of Policy Preferences" in chapter 3, where we summarized some standard economic models of policy cleavages as a prelude to our empirical analysis.

Trade Policy and Income

The key empirical implication of Stolper-Samuelson intuition is that the wage effects of trade-induced changes in product prices tend to depend on their sector bias. Any change that initially increases profits in a particular sector tends to raise the economywide wage for factor(s) employed relatively intensively in that sector. See Deardorff (1994) for a comprehensive survey of the many different theoretical statements of this theorem.

The Stolper-Samuelson discussion in chapter 3 presumed that all industries are tradable. However, in the United States today, more people work either in retail trade or in government at all levels than in all of manufacturing. Surely the logic of the Stolper-Samuelson model does not hold for countries like the United States, in which nearly 80 percent of the labor force is employed in largely nontradable sectors? Actually, it can very easily. With nontraded sectors, so long as the number of tradable goods is at least equal to the number of primary factors, national wages are still determined by the zero-profit conditions of the tradable sectors only. Nontraded product prices are endogenously determined by non-

Figure A.1 World wage pool: Manufacturing wages and population, 1994

wages (1994 dollars per hour)

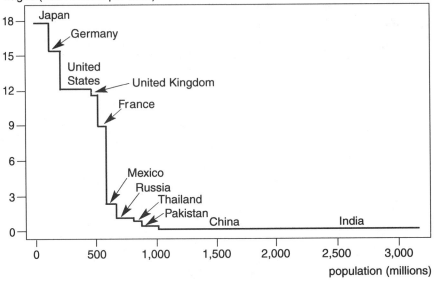

population (millions)

Source: Leamer (1998, updated).

traded production technology and by national wages, where these national wages are set by the product prices and technology levels in the tradable industries only.

What empirical evidence is there that the United States is well endowed with skilled labor relative to the rest of the world? Figure A.1 provides an illustration. The diagram shows the world wage pool in 1994 by plotting average manufacturing wages against population for many of the world's nations. The vertical axis shows each country's wage level in real 1994 US dollars; the horizontal axis shows each country's total population. Figure A.1 clearly shows dramatic differences: the world has some relatively small, high-wage countries like the United States along with many relatively large, low-wage countries (such as China). These cross-country differences in wages can result from many forces, but Leamer (1984) and others have shown that one important force is cross-country differences in relative labor supplies.

As for the implication that the United States protects its less-skill-intensive industries, figure A.2 shows evidence of this. For 1988, figure A.2 plots the level of industry tariff rates (measured as customs duties collected as a share of imports f.o.b.) on industry skill intensity measured as the ratio of nonproduction to production employment. The clear message of figure A.2 is that US tariffs and transportation costs were highest

Figure A.2   US tariffs are higher in less-skill-intensive sectors

industry tariff rate (percent)

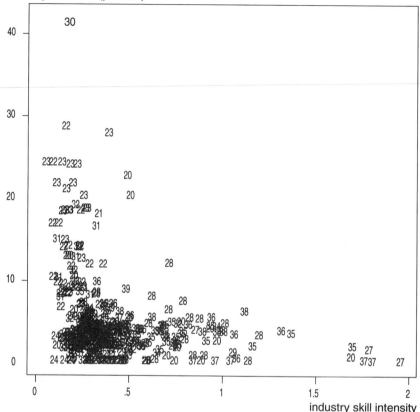

industry skill intensity

Note: Each observation is a four-digit SIC industry from the year 1988; for brevity, only the two-digit SIC code for each observation is reported. Industry skill intensity is the relative employment of nonproduction to production workers. Tariff rates are duties collected as a share of the customs value of imports. For readability, two zero-tariff skill-intensive industries are omitted: SIC 2721 (skill intensity of 4.83) and SIC 2731 (skill intensity of 3.25).

Source: Haskel and Slaughter (2000, figure 1a).

in the less-skill-intensive sectors, particularly in textiles (SIC 22), apparel (23), and footwear (31).[1]

Our analysis of trade policy preferences should not be interpreted as a direct test between the HO and RV models. A direct test would require data such as intersectoral factor movements and factor prices. There is

---

1. To examine the sector bias of barrier levels more formally, Haskel and Slaughter (2000) also regressed the levels of tariffs on the shares of more-skilled and less-skilled labor in total industry costs for 1974, 1979, and 1988. In every case tariffs were significantly concentrated in less-skill-intensive sectors.

nothing preventing preferences from being consistent with both models, not just one. The RV model can be characterized as a short-run version of the more long-run HO model. If there are meaningful barriers preventing worker mobility across industries, these barriers are likely to matter less over time. For example, it may be costly to lose industry-specific human capital today, but over many years this loss matters much less. In terms of the theory, Mayer (1974), Mussa (1974), and Neary (1978) compare wage changes in the two models, and Mussa (1978) formalizes how with intersectoral mobility costs an RV short run gradually becomes an HO long run. In reality, each model might be relevant over different time horizons. If individuals evaluate both short-run and long-run effects of trade liberalization, then trade policy preferences might depend on both factor type and industry of employment.[2]

Immigration Policy and Income

There is a good deal of empirical evidence on the skill mix of US immigrants in recent decades. For example, Borjas et al. (1997, 6) report that "on average, immigrants have fewer years of schooling than natives—a difference that has grown over the past two decades, as the mean years of schooling of the immigration population increased less rapidly than the mean years of schooling of natives. As a result, the immigrant contribution to the supply of skills has become increasingly concentrated in the lower educational categories." This skills gap between immigrants and natives does not address other interesting facts about the distribution of skills among immigrants. For example, Borjas et al. (1997, 7) show that the skill distribution of US immigration has been somewhat bimodal, with concentrations at both the high-skill and low-skill ends of the distribution.

To better understand immigration in the HO framework, start with two key assumptions. First, above and beyond the intersectoral factor mobility discussed earlier, there is interregional labor mobility as well: thanks to sufficient mobility of natives (and immigrants on arrival), there are no geographically segmented "local" labor markets. The second key assumption is that there are more tradable products (i.e., sectors) than primary factors of production, with products differentiated by their factor intensities. Multiple products are essential for establishing many fundamental trade theory results, such as comparative advantage.

With these assumptions, in equilibrium a country chooses (via the decentralized optimization of firms) the output mix that maximizes

---

2. Another way both models might accurately describe the economy is that within some time frame specificity might vary across units in the economy (such as industries or factor types). Thus, within the same time frame both the HO and RV models might apply, each to different parts of the economy. Alt et al. (1999) find support for this perspective in their study of firm lobbying behavior in Norway.

national income subject to the constraints of world product prices, national factor supplies, and national technology. This output mix consists of both the products that actually get produced and the quantities of production. In turn, this output mix helps determine the country's national factor prices. The general intuition is that the technology parameters and world price for each produced sector help determine national wages. The standard case was discussed in the previous section: when the country makes at least as many products as the number of primary factors, equilibrium wages are a function of just the world prices and technology parameters of the produced sectors. These wages do not depend on the prices and technology of the nonproduced sectors. They also do not depend directly on the level of endowments (only indirectly through the endowments' role in selecting the product mix).

Immigration's wage effects depend on the initial product mix, on the size of the immigration shock, and on whether the country's economy is large enough to have any influence on world product prices. Consider the standard case, where the initial output mix is sufficiently diversified that wages depend on just world prices and technology.

In this case, "sufficiently small" immigration is absorbed by the country changing its output mix as predicted by the Rybczynski (1955) theorem: the same products are produced, but output tends to increase in the less-skill-intensive sectors and to decrease in the more-skill-intensive sectors. How exactly does this happen? With the change in factor supplies available to hire, firms will have an incentive to produce more output of those products that employ relatively intensively the now more-abundant factors. Whether wages change depends on whether the country is big or small. If the country is small, world prices do not change and thus there are no wage effects. The cross-industry shifts in output, thanks to differences in factor intensity across industries, generate economywide shifts in factor demand that just match the economywide change in factor supplies. Leamer and Levinsohn (1995) call this insensitivity of national wages to changes in national factor supplies the factor-price-insensitivity (FPI) theorem. On the other hand, if the country is large, then wages do change via the Stolper-Samuelson process: the relative price of less-skill-intensive products declines, which lowers wages for less-skilled workers and raises wages for more-skilled workers.

With "sufficiently large" immigration shocks, national wages do change. Large enough shocks induce the country to make a different set of products, which entails a different set of world prices and technology parameters and thus different wages. This absorption of large shocks via changes in both output mix and wages holds whether the country is large or small: in either case wage inequality rises.

It is worth emphasizing the somewhat counterintuitive idea of FPI, with which immigrants might generate zero wage pressures thanks to changes in output mix. Do these changes actually happen in the real world? Little empirical research has examined this (see Hanson and Slaughter 2000). Much of the empirical work on the labor-market impacts of immigration have, implicitly or explicitly, used the factor-proportions or area-studies frameworks. Studies using the former include those of Borjas et al. (1996; 1997),which calculate immigration-induced shifts in national factor proportions and then infer the resulting national wage changes. A large number of studies have used the area-studies framework, including Card (1990), Altonji and Card (1991), and LaLonde and Topel (1991). These studies generally test for correlations between immigrant flows into local labor markets and local native wages. Again, the key difference between these two frameworks is the geographic extent of immigrants' wage effects. In a national labor market, immigrants' wage pressures spread beyond gateway communities. Natives can leave gateway communities when immigrants arrive; immigrants can move on to other communities; or natives can choose not to enter gateway communities as planned preimmigration. In cases between these two extremes, immigrants affect wages everywhere, but to a greater extent in gateway labor markets.

Other Considerations: Trade Policy and Asset Values

Many assets do fit easily into the HO framework. Some assets are currently employed by firms as factors of production—for example, machine tools and office buildings. These assets earn rates of return that are determined just as wages are, as outlined above. In turn, these rates of return are an important determinant of asset prices.[3] Another kind of asset that fits into standard trade models is currently produced goods such as automobiles. Their domestic prices are set just like those of other nonasset products, as some combination of world prices and domestic trade barriers.

The assumption that construction adds very little to housing stocks is borne out in the data. The US Census Bureau estimates that on 1 July 1996, the total US housing stock was 110 million housing units (US Census Bureau, Estimates of Housing Units, Households, Households, by Age of Householder, and Persons per Household [August 1997], http://www.census.gov/population/www/estimates/housing.html [October 1997]). In 1996, approximately 1.3 million new homes were constructed nationwide. According to averages from the 1980s, approximately 0.3 million existing homes would have become uninhabitable that year due to demolition, disasters, and other causes. Thus, the net construction rate

---

3. There is a well-developed literature analyzing how these productive assets accumulate over time in open trading economies. See, for example, the surveys of Findlay (1984) and Smith (1984).

in 1996 was about 1 million new homes—0.9 percent of the existing stock. Also, the Census Bureau estimates that nationwide in 1996, an average of 8.33 months passed from the time a residential construction permit was issued to the time construction was completed.

For the average US household in 1990, the gross value of the primary residence accounted for nearly 90 percent of total household assets (Caplin et al. 1997). For the median US homeowner in all age groups in 1986, housing equity accounted for more than half of his or her total wealth (Skinner 1994). So even though the NES survey data cover only one asset, it is the single largest asset for a significant share of the population.

Research in the regional-economics literature has documented an empirical link between local industry mix and local housing prices. Case and Mayer (1996) found that in the Boston area during the 1980s, average house prices rose less in housing jurisdictions with a larger share of residents employed in manufacturing in 1980. They hypothesize that this empirical link reflects "displaced manufacturing workers. . .reducing their demand for housing" (391).

Note that the link between trade and asset values operates independently of trade's effect on labor incomes. People's economic welfare depends on both income and asset holdings, and freer trade might affect these two channels differently. Consider a more-skilled homeowner in Gary, Indiana, a city with production very concentrated in a sector with comparative disadvantage, steel. This person might support freer trade through the income channel but oppose it through the asset channel. We distinguish between these two links in the data analysis.

Appendix B
Data Description

The survey data presented in chapter 2 are from the Public Opinion Databank at the Roper Center for Public Opinion Research. The original sources for each survey are listed with each question.

The data used in the analysis in chapter 3 were obtained from the following sources.

- National Bureau of Economic Research, Manufacturing Industry Database, http://www.nber.org/nberces.

- Sapiro, Virginia, Steven J. Rosenstone, Warren E. Miller, and the National Election Studies. 1998. American National Election Studies, 1948-97 [CD-ROM], ed. ICPSR. Ann Arbor, MI: Inter-University Consortium for Political and Social Research [producer and distributor].

- United States Bureau of the Census. 1992. Census of Manufactures, 1992. Washington: US Government Printing Office.

- United States Bureau of the Census. 1994. State and Metropolitan Area Data Book, 1994. Washington: US Government Printing Office.

- United States Department of Commerce, Bureau of Economic Analysis, Survey of Current Business and Trade and Employment, various years. Washington: US Government Printing Office.

- United States Department of Labor, Bureau of Labor Statistics. 1992, 1994, and 1996. Unpublished tabulations from the current population survey, table A-26, 1992, 1994, and 1996 annual averages.

- United States International Trade Commission. 1997. Unpublished data file on US tariffs collected in 1992.

Sector Net Export Share

To construct this variable, we obtained Robert C. Feenstra's data from the NBER on 1992 manufacturing exports, imports, and value of shipments at the four-digit Standard Industrial Classification (SIC) (revision 2) level. To cover all truly tradable sectors, we obtained similar data for agriculture and tradable services from various BEA sources. All these data were concorded to the 1980 Census Industrial Classification (CIC) industries, and then for each industry we calculated *Sector Net Export Share* as exports minus imports divided by value of shipments. For all nontradable sectors we set this variable equal to zero.

Sector Tariff

To construct this variable, we obtained data from the ITC on 1992 tariff duties collected and customs-value imports at the four-digit SIC (revision 3) level.[1] We concorded these tariff and import values to the 1980 CIC industries, and then for each industry we calculated an effective tariff rate by dividing tariffs value by imports value.

High-Immigration MSA

First, we defined local labor markets two ways: by a combination of metropolitan statistical areas (MSAs) and counties, and by states. In our MSA/county definition, each MSA (with all its constituent cities and counties) is a separate labor market; for individuals living outside an MSA, the labor market is the county of residence. Following the extensive use of MSAs in area-analysis studies and Bartel's (1989) finding that immigrants arrive mostly into cities, we prefer the MSA/county definition but tried states for robustness. Second, for each definition of local labor markets we tried three different definitions of a high-immigration labor market: 5 percent, 10 percent, and 20 percent shares of immigrants in the local population. These immigration and labor force data are from the 1990 census as reported by the US Census Bureau (*State and Metropolitan Area Data Book*, 1994). Altogether, for each of our six primary measures we construct a dichotomous variable, *High-Immigration MSA*, equal to 1 for residents in high-immigration labor markets. In the tables we report

---

1. We thank Michael Ferrantino at the US International Trade Commission for helping us obtain these data.

results for our preferred measure, the MSA/county 10 percent definition. Alternative measures are discussed in the robustness checks reviewed in chapter 3.[2]

Noneconomic Variables

Gender is a dichotomous variable equal to 1 for females. *Age* is a continuous variable (for the trade analysis it is divided into three dichotomous measures—Age 18-29, Age 30-44, and Age 45-59—and a residual category). *Race* is a dichotomous variable equal to 1 if the respondent is African-American. For ethnicity we constructed the dichotomous variable *Hispanic*, equal to 1 if the individual self-identifies with a Hispanic ethnic group. *Immigrant* is a dichotomous variable equal to 1 if the respondent or his or her parents were immigrants into the United States. *Party Identification* is a categorical variable ranging from 1 for "strong Democrat" to 7 for "strong Republican." Finally, *Ideology* is a categorical variable ranging from 1 for "extremely liberal" to 7 for "extremely conservative." In addition to these variables, for certain specifications in the robustness checks we included additional regressors, which are discussed in the text.

2. In 1990, immigrants accounted for 7.9 percent of the US population. Thus, our 5 percent cutoff might seem too low, but for the sake of completeness we tried it anyway. Also, the 1990 census MSA data are organized by 1990 MSA definitions, but the 1992 NES survey locates individuals by 1980 MSA definitions. Using unpublished information on 1980-90 MSA changes obtained from Census Bureau officials, we corrected discrepancies as best we could.

Appendix C
Multiple Imputation Methodology

The data constructed for analysis in this study are not fully observed. The sources of "missingness" range from survey respondents' refusal to answer particular questions in some surveys to the suppression of data by national agencies to avoid identifying particular commercial establishments. Incomplete data, whatever the source, can create a number of serious problems for making valid statistical inferences.

For example, the most common approach in the social sciences to multivariate analyses of incomplete data is to drop cases that have any missing data and analyze only the complete cases. This standard approach, known as listwise deletion, can create two major problems. One is the inefficiency of throwing away information relevant to the statistical inferences being made. The other is that inferences from listwise deletion estimation can be biased if the observed data differ systematically from the unobserved data. In this study, since "missingness" in particular variables ranged from none to nearly 75 percent, inefficiency was clearly a concern. Moreover, *ex ante* there was little reason to believe that data were missing completely at random, so employing a listwise deletion approach risked bias as well.

Alternatives to listwise deletion for dealing with missing data have been developed in recent years. The most general and extensively researched approach is multiple imputation (King et al. 2001; Schafer 1997; Little and Rubin 1987; Rubin 1987). Multiple imputation makes a much weaker assumption than listwise deletion about the process generating the missing data. Rather than assuming that the unobserved data are missing completely at random, multiple imputation is consistent and gives correct uncertainty estimates if the data are missing randomly conditional on the data included in the imputation procedures.[1] Moreover, multiple imputation offers important advantages over ad hoc procedures for dealing with missing data. Imputing sample averages on a variable-by-variable basis biases estimates and standard errors toward zero. Imputing predicted values from regression models tends to inflate sample correlations and thus bias estimates away from zero. Given all these advantages of multiple imputation, we use this estimation methodology.

The remainder of this appendix provides the specific details of the imputation procedures used in the trade and immigration analyses.

Trade

After the variables described in chapter 3 were constructed and combined into individual-level data sets for each cross-sectional survey, there was a significant amount of missing data. In the NES survey some individuals did not report either occupation, education, or industry of employment, which prevented the construction of some of the factor-income trade-exposure variables for these people. The most serious missing-data problem arose from the homeowners' exposure variables that were constructed for the asset analysis we presented in the section Asset Ownership and Trade Policy Preferences. In fact, the structure of the missing-data problems differed between the 1992 data, for which the asset analysis was conducted, and the 1996 data, for which it was not. Consequently, we used slightly different procedures for the imputations in each year and describe them separately.

For 1992, the first step in our multiple imputation procedures was to impute missing observations for *County Exposure 1* and *County Exposure*

---

1. The multiple imputation procedures used in this study actually require that two conditions be met. First, as discussed in the text, the probability that a data cell is missing may depend on observed data included in the imputation model but must be independent of unobserved data. In the imputation literature, this assumption is known as Missing at Random (MAR). Note that this assumption is weaker than assuming that the data are Missing Completely at Random (MCAR), which means that the probability that a data cell is missing does not depend on any data, whether observed or not. Further, the analyst can make the MAR assumption more reasonable by including a large number of variables in the imputation model. For example, even if less-skilled respondents in the trade opinion analysis are less likely to report their occupations, the MAR assumption is not violated if the other observed data correlated with skill account for this aspect of the missingness mechanism. The second condition is that the parameters describing the data are distinct from those describing the missingness mechanism in the data. Schafer contends that in many situations similar to the analyses in this study distinctness is a reasonable assumption, as knowing the data parameters provides little information about the parameters describing the patterns of missingness in the data set (1997, 11). If the missingness problem meets these two conditions, it is called ignorable and the imputation methods used in this study are appropriate. These assumptions have been shown to be reasonable in many studies similar to the one here that include rich data sets with many covariates to include in the imputation model.

2. Imputations were based on dozens of variables selected for their sample correlation with the missing variables. For example, for imputation of *County Exposure 1* and *County Exposure 2*, county employment in textiles was used because it had one of the highest sample correlations with the county-exposure variables. Altogether, 10 complete county data sets were imputed.

The exact algorithm used for these imputations is a data augmentation method known by the acronym IP because it involves two key steps: the imputation step and the posterior step. The goal of the imputation procedure is to estimate a set of parameters (means and variance/covariances of all the variables) that can be used to create the 10 imputed data sets. In this application, it is assumed that the data have a joint multivariate normal distribution. Consequently, IP employs an iterative sampling scheme in which in the first step imputations are drawn from the multivariate normal conditional predictive distribution of the missing data. This distribution depends on the observed data and the assumed or current value of the complete data parameters. In the second step, a new value of the complete data parameters is drawn from its posterior distribution, which is conditioned on the observed data and the current values of the imputations for the missing data. This posterior step is a simulation from the normal inverted-Wishart distribution. Repeating this iterative sampling scheme produces stochastic subsequences that converge on the stationary predictive distribution for the missing values and the stationary posterior distribution of the complete data parameters.[2]

For the county data set we ran 5,000 iterations of IP and then ran 1,000 more creating an imputed data set every 100 iterations of these last 1,000. The preliminary iterations ensure that sequences have converged to their stationary distributions. After creating the 10 complete county data sets, we merged the NES survey data (including the constructed skill measures and industry measures) with *County Exposure 1* and *County Exposure 2*. The resulting 10 data sets still had substantial amounts of missing individual-level data, however. Consequently, for each of these 10 data sets we ran separate iterations of IP in order to impute values for the missing survey data. We found that 2,100 preliminary iterations were more than sufficient for these data sets. An imputation was saved on the last iteration of each of the 10 cases to create the 10 final data sets with no missing data at all. Each of these final data sets for 1992 contains 1,736 observations, equal to the actual number of individuals in the NES survey either supporting or opposing more trade restrictions.[3] Also, each data set contains

---

2. See section 3.4 in Schafer (1997) for a complete description of IP. Also, our methodology assumes that all variables are normally distributed. To make the data fit this assumption more closely, we redefined each county-level variable to equal the natural log of the variable plus one.

3. All the main results reported are qualitatively the same for the case where imputations are also made by treating as missing data the fact that some respondents did not express

the exact same nonimputed information (i.e., all observations for the variable *Trade Opinion* plus the nonimputed observations for all the trade-exposure variables). They differ only in their imputed values for missing data.

For 1996, the first step in the multiple imputation procedure was to create imputations in the missing-data cells for all the individual-level variables (since no county-level analysis was conducted for these data, it was not necessary to break down the imputation procedures to two levels of aggregation). We based the imputations for the 1996 data on 26 variables. These variables included all those used in the analysis as well as additional information that would be helpful in predicting the missing data. Altogether we imputed 10 complete individual-level data sets. The final data sets contain 846 completed observations, equal to the actual number of individuals in the NES survey either supporting or opposing more trade restrictions. The imputation model was multivariate normal with a slight ridge prior. The algorithm used to implement this model is known by the acronym EMis, because to generate imputations it combines a well-known expectation maximization missing-data algorithm with a round of importance sampling. King et al. (2001) provide a complete explanation of the use of this algorithm for missing-data problems.

The second step in the multiple imputation analysis was to run various logit models separately on each of the 10 final data sets for each year, and the final step was to combine the 10 sets of estimation results for each specification to obtain a single set of estimated parameter means and variances. The single set of estimated means is simply the arithmetic average of the 10 different estimation results. The single set of estimated variances consists of two parts. The "within" component is simply the arithmetic average of the 10 estimated variances. This accounts for the ordinary within-sample variation. The "between" component is the variance of the estimated parameter means among the imputed data sets. See King et al. (2001) and Schafer (1997) for a complete description of the final multiple-imputation step.

Immigration

After the variables described in chapter 3 were constructed and combined into individual-level data sets for each cross-sectional survey, there was a

---

a trade policy opinion. For this analysis the multiple imputation procedures created 10 data sets of 2,485 observations, equal to the total number of respondents in the NES survey. In addition, all the main results are qualitatively the same using the listwise deletion method for missing data. Finally, we explicitly modeled whether or not the respondent offered an opinion simultaneously with the determinants of the opinions given using a Heckman probit selection model. Our skill and industry findings were robust to this specification, and the analysis revealed significantly lower levels of political awareness among those who did not answer the question.

significant amount of missing data. Across the range of models estimated, when we simply dropped observations with any missing data we generally lost 25 to 45 percent of the total observations.

The first step in the multiple imputation procedure was to create imputations in the missing-data cells for all the variables. We based the imputations for the 1992, 1994, and 1996 data on 36, 28, and 26 variables, respectively, selected from the NES surveys. These variables included all those used in the analysis as well as additional information from each survey that would be helpful in predicting the missing data. Altogether we imputed 10 complete individual-level data sets for each year. The final data sets contain completed observations equal to the actual number of individuals in each NES survey. The imputation model was multivariate normal with a slight ridge prior. The algorithm used to implement this model is known by the acronym EMis, because to generate imputations it combines a well-known expectation maximization missing data algorithm with a round of importance sampling. King et al. (2001) provide a complete explanation of the use of this algorithm for missing data problems.

The second step in the multiple imputation analysis was to run various ordered probit models separately on each of the 10 final data sets for each survey year. The last multiple imputation step was to combine the 10 sets of estimation results for each specification.

Appendix D
Further Evidence of the Skills-Preferences Cleavage

The skills-preferences cleavage described in chapter 3 is corroborated by surveys other than the NES surveys. Some surveys in the data we present in chapter 2 report responses broken down by skill measures such as educational attainment or household income. Survey responses grouped solely by skills must be interpreted cautiously: these groups alone do not control for other possible sources of preferences cleavages that might be correlated with skills, and sample differences across skill groupings need not be statistically significant. That said, these surveys support our findings on the skills-preferences cleavage originally presented in the multivariate analysis of Scheve and Slaughter (2001a, b).

Here are three examples. All repeat questions of the "is trade good or bad" variety, like those presented in chapter 2. The pattern is clear: among respondents with less education, opposition to trade seems much stronger.

Question: Do you think it should be the policy of the country to restrict foreign imports in order to protect jobs and domestic industries, or do you think there should be no restrictions on the sale of foreign products in order to permit the widest choice and the lowest prices for the consumer?

"Restrict" responses:
Those with advanced degree: 53%
Those with college degree: 61%
Those with some college: 68%
Those with high school degree: 77%
Those with less than high school: 73%

Source: Los Angeles Times, February 1992

Question: What do you think foreign trade means for America? Do you see foreign trade more as an opportunity for economic growth through increased US exports, or a threat to the economy from foreign imports?

"Opportunity" responses:
                     Those with advanced degree: 73%
                     Those with college degree: 75%
                     Those with some college: 57%
                     Those with high school degree: 42%
                     Those with less than high school: 37%

Source: CNN/*USA Today*, November 1994

Question: As you may know, with freer trade, jobs are often lost due to imports from other countries, while new jobs are created when the US exports more products to other countries. I'd like you to imagine in one industry some jobs are lost because of foreign competition, while in a different industry an equal number are created, but these new jobs pay higher wages. Which of the following statements do you agree with the most?
                     A: Even if the new jobs that come from freer trade pay higher wages, overall it is not worth all the disruption of people losing their jobs.
                     B: It is better to have the higher-paying jobs, and the people who lost their jobs can eventually find new ones.

"A" responses: Those with college degree or higher: 33%
                     Those with high school degree: 65%
                     Those with less than high school: 66%

Source: Program on International Policy Attitudes, October 1999

References

Abraham, Katharine, James Spletzer, and Jay Stewart. 1999. Why Do Different Wage Series Tell Different Stories? *American Economic Review* 89, no. 2 (May): 34-39.

Aldrich, John, Claire Kramer, Peter Lange, Renan Levine, John Rattliff, Laura Stephenson, and Elizabeth Zechmeister. 1999a. Job Insecurity and Globalization: Evidence from Europe. Paper presented at the 1999 annual meeting of the American Political Science Association, Atlanta (August).

Aldrich, John, Claire Kramer, Peter Lange, Renan Levine, John Rattliff, Laura Stephenson, and Elizabeth Zechmeister. 1999b. Racing the Titanic: Globalization, Insecurity, and American Democracy. Paper presented at the 1999 annual meeting of the American Political Science Association, Atlanta (August).

Alt, James E. 1979. *The Politics of Economic Decline: Economic Management and Political Behavior in Britain since 1964.* Cambridge, England: Cambridge University Press.

Alt, James E. 1991. Ambiguous Intervention: The Role of Government Action in Public Evaluation of the Economy. In *Economics and Politics: The Calculus of Support*, ed. Helmut Norpoth, Michael S. Lewis-Beck, and Jean-Dominique Lafay. Ann Arbor: University of Michigan Press.

Alt, James E., Fredrik Carlsen, Per Heum, and Kåre Johansen. 1999. Asset Specificity and the Political Behavior of Firms: Lobbying for Subsidies in Norway. *International Organization* 53, no. 1 (Winter): 99-116.

Altonji, Joseph, and David Card. 1991. The Effects of Immigration on the Labor Market Outcomes of Less-Skilled Natives. In *Immigration, Trade, and the Labor Market*, ed. John Abowd and Richard Freeman. Chicago: University of Chicago Press.

Alvarez, R. Michael. 1997. *Information and Elections.* Ann Arbor: University of Michigan Press.

Alvarez, R. Michael, and John Brehm. 1995. American Ambivalence toward Abortion Policy: A Heteroskedastic Probit Method for Assessing Conflicting Values. *American Journal of Political Science* 39, no. 4 (November): 1055-82.

Alvarez, R. Michael, and John Brehm. 1997. Are Americans Ambivalent towards Racial Policies? *American Journal of Political Science* 41, no. 2 (April): 345-74.

Anderson, Christopher, and Karl Kaltenthaler. 1996. The Dynamic of Public Opinion toward European Integration, 1973-1993. *European Journal of International Relations* 2, no. 2: 175-99.

Baldwin, Robert E., and Glen G. Cain. 2000. Shifts in US Relative Wages: The Role of Trade, Technology, and Factor Endowments. *Review of Economics and Statistics* 82, no. 4, November 580-95.

Baldwin, Robert E., and Christopher S. Magee. 2000. *Congressional Trade Votes: From NAFTA Approval to Fast-Track Defeat*. POLICY ANALYSES IN INTERNATIONAL ECONOMICS 59. Washington: Institute for International Economics.

Bartel, Ann. 1989. Where Do the New US Immigrants Live? *Journal of Labor Economics* 7, no. 4: 371-91.

Bhagwati, Jagdish. 1991. *Free Traders and Free Immigrationists: Strangers or Friends?* Russell Sage Foundation Working Paper. New York: Russell Sage Foundation.

Blanchflower, Danny, and Matthew J. Slaughter. 1999. The Causes and Consequences of Changing Earnings Inequality. In *Growing Apart: The Causes and Consequences of Global Wage Inequality*, ed. Albert Fishlow and Karen Parker. New York: Council on Foreign Relations, 69-94.

Blonigen, Bruce A., and Matthew J. Slaughter. 2000. US Skill Upgrading and Inward Foreign Direct Investment. *Review of Economics and Statistics*, 83(2), May.

Borjas, George J. 1999. *Heaven's Door: Immigration Policy and the American Economy*. Princeton, NJ: Princeton University Press.

Borjas, George J. 1994. The Economics of Immigration. *Journal of Economic Literature* 32 (December): 1667-1717.

Borjas, George J., Richard B. Freeman, and Lawrence F. Katz. 1997. How Much Do Immigration and Trade Affect Labor Market Outcomes? *Brookings Papers on Economic Activity* 1: 1-90. Washington: Brookings Institution.

Borjas, George J., Richard B. Freeman, and Lawrence F. Katz. 1996. Searching for the Effect of Immigration on the Labor Market. *American Economic Review* 86, no. 2: 247-51.

Busch, Marc, and Eric Reinhardt. 2000. Geography, International Trade, and Political Mobilization in US Industries. *American Journal of Political Science*, 44(4), October.

Caplin, Andrew, Sewin Chan, Charles Freeman, and Joseph Tracy. 1997. *Housing Partnerships: A New Approach to a Market at a Crossroads*. Cambridge, MA: MIT Press.

Card, David. 1990. The Impact of the Mariel Boatlift on the Miami Labor Market. *Industrial and Labor Relations Review* 43, no. 2: 245-57.

Card, David. 1997. *Immigrant Inflows, Native Outflows, and the Local Labor Market Impacts of Higher Immigration*. NBER Working Papers 5927. Cambridge, MA: National Bureau of Economic Research.

Case, Karl E., and Christopher J. Mayer. 1996. Housing Price Dynamics Within a Metropolitan Area. *Regional Science and Urban Economics* 26: 387-407.

Chappell, Henry W., Jr., and William R. Keech. 1985. A New View of Political Accountability for Economic Performance. *American Political Science Review* 79, no. 1 (March): 10-27.

Citrin, Jack, Donald Green, Christopher Muste, and Cara Wong. 1997. Public Opinion toward Immigration Reform: The Role of Economic Motivation. *Journal of Politics* 59, no. 3: 858-81.

Conover, Pamela Johnston, and Stanley Feldman. 1981. The Origins and Meanings of Liberal/Conservative Self-Identification. *American Journal of Political Science* 25, no. 4 (November): 617-45.

Conover, Pamela Johnston, Stanley Feldman, and Kathleen Knight. 1987. The Personal and Political Underpinnings of Economic Forecasts. *American Journal of Political Science* 31, no. 3 (August): 559-83.

Converse, Philip E. 1964. The Nature of Belief Systems in Mass Publics. In *Ideology and Discontent*, ed. David Apter. New York: Free Press.

Converse, Philip, and Gregory Markus. 1979. Plus Ça Change: The CPS Election Study Panel. *American Political Science Review* 73, no. 1 (March): 32-49.

Deardorff, Alan V. 1994. Overview of the Stolper-Samuelson Theorem. In *The Stolper-Samuelson Theorem: A Golden Jubilee*, ed. Alan V. Deardorff and Robert M. Stern. Ann Arbor: University of Michigan Press.

Delli Carpini, Michael X., and Scott Keeter. 1996. *What Americans Know about Politics and Why It Matters*. New Haven: Yale University Press.

Destler, I. M. 1995. *American Trade Politics*, 3rd ed. Washington: Institute for International Economics; New York: Twentieth Century Fund.

Downs, Anthony. 1957. *An Economic Theory of Democracy*. New York: Harper Collins.

Eichenberg, Richard, and Russell Dalton. 1993. Europeans and the European Community: The Dynamics of Public Support for European Integration. *International Organization* 47, no. 4 (Autumn): 507-34.

Espenshade, Thomas J., and Katherine Hempstead. 1996. Contemporary American Attitudes toward US Immigration. *International Migration Review* 30, no. 2: 535-70.

Feenstra, Robert C., and Gordon H. Hanson. 1999. The Impact of Outsourcing and High-Technology Capital on Wages. *Quarterly Journal of Economics* 114, no. 3 (August): 907-40.

Fernandez, Raquel, and Dani Rodrik. 1991. Resistance to Reform: Status Quo Bias in the Presence of Individual-Specific Uncertainty. *American Economic Review* 81, no. 5 (December): 1146-55.

Findlay, Ronald. 1984. Growth and Development in Trade Models. In *Handbook of International Economics*, vol. 1, ed. Ronald W. Jones and Peter B. Kenen. Amsterdam: Elsevier Science Publishers.

Fiorina, Morris. 1981. *Retrospective Voting in American National Elections*. New Haven: Yale University Press.

Freeman, Richard. 1995. Are Your Wages Set in Beijing? *Journal of Economic Perspectives* 9, no. 3 (Summer): 15-32.

Friedberg, Rachel, and Jennifer Hunt. 1995. The Impact of Immigrants on Host Country Wages, Employment, and Growth. *Journal of Economic Perspectives* 9, no. 2: 23-44.

Frieden, Jeffry A. 1991. Invested Interests: The Politics of National Economic Policies in a World of Global Finance. *International Organization* 45, no. 4 (Autumn): 425-52.

Friedman, Thomas L. 2000. *The Lexus and the Olive Tree*. New York: Farrar Straus & Giroux.

Gabel, Matthew. 1998a. *Interests and Integration: Market Liberalization, Public Opinion, and the European Union*. Ann Arbor: University of Michigan Press.

Gabel, Matthew. 1998b. Economic Integration and Mass Politics: Market Liberalization and Public Attitudes in the European Union. *American Journal of Political Science* 42, no. 3 (July): 936-53.

Garrett, Geoffrey. 1998. *Partisan Politics in the Global Economy*. Cambridge, England: Cambridge University Press.

Graham, Edward M. 2000. *Fighting the Wrong Enemy: Antiglobal Activists and Multinational Enterprises*. Washington: Institute for International Economics.

Greider, William. 1997. *One World, Ready or Not: The Manic Logic of Global Capitalism*. New York: Simon and Schuster.

Hanson, Gordon H., and Matthew J. Slaughter. 2000. Labor-Market Adjustment in Open Economies: Evidence from US States. *Journal of International Economics*, forthcoming.

Haskel, Jonathan E., and Matthew J. Slaughter. 2000. *Have Falling Tariffs and Transportation Costs Raised US Wage Inequality?* NBER Working Papers 7539. Cambridge, MA: National Bureau of Economic Research.

Hiscox, Michael. 1997. *The Trade War at Home: Factor Mobility, International Trade, and Political Coalitions in Democracies*. Ph.D. dissertation, Department of Government, Harvard University.

Irwin, Douglas A. 1994. The Political Economy of Free Trade: Voting in the British General Election of 1906. *Journal of Law and Economics* 37 (April): 75-108.

Irwin, Douglas A. 1996. Industry or Class Cleavages over Trade Policy? Evidence from the British General Election of 1923. In *The Political Economy of Trade Policy: Papers in Honor of Jagdish Bhagwati*, ed. Robert C. Feenstra, Gene M. Grossman, and Douglas A. Irwin. Cambridge, MA: MIT Press.

Johnson, George. 1997. Changes in Earnings Inequality: The Role of Demand Shifts. *Journal of Economic Perspectives* 11, no. 2 (Spring): 41-54.

Kapstein, Ethan. 1999. *Sharing the Wealth: Workers and the World Economy.* New York: W. W. Norton.

Katz, Lawrence F., and Alan B. Krueger. 1999. The High-Pressure US Labor Market. *Brookings Papers on Economic Activity*, 1, 1-87.

Keohane, Robert O., and Joseph S. Nye. 2000. Globalization: What's New? What's Not? (And So What?). *Foreign Policy* 118 (Spring): 104-19.

Kessler, Alan. 1998. Distributional Coalitions, Trade, and the Politics of Postwar American Immigration. Paper presented at the 1998 annual meeting of the American Political Science Association, Boston (August).

Key, V. O., and Milton Cummings. 1966. *The Responsible Electorate: Rationality in Presidential Voting, 1936-1960.* Cambridge, MA: Harvard University Press.

King, Gary, James Honaker, Anne Joseph, and Kenneth F. Scheve. 2001. Analyzing Incomplete Political Science Data: An Alternative Algorithm for Multiple Imputation. *American Political Science Review*, forthcoming.

Kramer, Gerald. 1971. Short-term Fluctuations in US Voting Behavior, 1896-1964. *American Political Science Review* 65: 131-45.

Krugman, Paul R. 1992. *The Age of Diminished Expectations.* Cambridge, MA: MIT Press.

Lane, Robert. 1962. *Political Ideology: Why the Common Man Believes What He Does.* New York: Free Press.

LaLonde, Robert, and Robert Topel. 1991. Labor Market Adjustments to Increased Immigration." In *Immigration, Trade, and the Labor Market,* ed. John Abowd and Richard Freeman. Chicago: University of Chicago Press.

Lawrence, Robert Z., and Matthew J. Slaughter. 1993. International Trade and American Wages in the 1980s: Giant Sucking Sound or Small Hiccup? *Brookings Papers on Economic Activity: Microeconomics* 2: 161-211.

Leamer, Edward E. 1984. *Sources of International Comparative Advantage.* Cambridge, MA: MIT Press.

Leamer, Edward E. 1998. In Search of Stolper-Samuelson Linkages between International Trade and Lower Wages. In *Imports, Exports, and the American Worker,* ed. Susan M. Collins. Washington: Brookings Institution Press.

Leamer, Edward E., and James Levinsohn. 1995. International Trade Theory: The Evidence. In *Handbook on International Economics,* vol. 3, ed. Gene M. Grossman and Kenneth Rogoff. Amsterdam: North Holland Press.

Little, Roderick J. A., and Donald B. Rubin. 1987. *Statistical Analysis With Missing Data.* New York: J. Wiley & Sons.

Lupia, Arthur. 1992. Busy Voters, Agenda Control, and the Power of Information. *American Political Science Review* 86, no. 2 (June): 390-403.

Lupia, Arthur. 1994. Shortcuts versus Encyclopedias: Information and Voting Behavior in California Insurance Reform Elections. *American Political Science Review* 88, no. 1 (March): 63-76.

Lupia, Arthur, and Mathew D. McCubbins. 1998. *The Democratic Dilemma: Can Citizens Learn What They Need to Know?* Cambridge, England: Cambridge University Press.

MacKuen, Michael B., Robert S. Erikson, and James A. Stimson. 1992. Peasants or Bankers? The American Electorate and the US Economy. *American Political Science Review* 86, no. 3 (September): 597-611.

Mayer, Wolfgang. 1974. Short-Run and Long-Run Equilibrium for a Small Open Economy. *Journal of Political Economy* 82, no. 5: 955-67.

Midford, P. 1993. International Trade and Domestic Politics: Improving on Rogowski's Model of Political Alignments. *International Organization* 47, no. 4: 535-64.

Mussa, Michael. 1974. Tariffs and the Distribution of Income: The Importance of Factor Specificity, Substitutability, and Intensity in the Short and Long Run. *Journal of Political Economy* 82, no. 6: 1191-1203.

Mussa, Michael. 1978. Dynamic Adjustment in the Heckscher-Ohlin-Samuelson Model. *Journal of Political Economy* 86 (October): 775-91.

Neary, J. Peter. 1978. Short-Run Capital Specificity and the Pure Theory of International Trade. *The Economic Journal* 88 (September): 448-510.

Nie, Norman H., Sidney Verba, and John Petrocik. 1979. *The Changing American Voter.* Cambridge, MA: Harvard University Press.

Popkin, Samuel L. 1991. *The Reasoning Voter.* Chicago: University of Chicago Press.

Program on International Policy Attitudes [PIPA]. 2000. *Americans on Globalization: A Study of US Public Attitudes.* Center on Policy Attitudes and Center for International and Security Studies, School of Public Affairs, University of Maryland. http://www.pipa.org/OnlineReports/Globalization/pdf/globalization.pdf (June 2000).

Prusa, Thomas J. 1999. *On the Spread and Impact of Antidumping.* NBER Working Papers 7404. Cambridge, MA: National Bureau of Economic Research.

Rahn, Wendy M., John H. Aldrich, and Eugene Borgida. 1994. Individual and Contextual Variations in Political Candidate Appraisal. *American Political Science Review* 88, no. 1 (March): 193-99.

Richardson, J. David. 1995. Income Inequality and Trade: How to Think, What to Conclude. *Journal of Economic Perspectives* 9, no. 3 (Summer): 33-55.

Richardson, J. David, and Karin Rindal. 1995. *Why Exports Really Matter!* Washington: Institute for International Economics and The Manufacturing Institute.

Richardson, J. David, and Karin Rindal. 1996. *Why Exports Matter: More!* Washington: Institute for International Economics and The Manufacturing Institute.

Rodrik, Dani. 1995. Political Economy of Trade Policy. In *Handbook of International Economics,* vol. 3, ed. Gene Grossman and Ken Rogoff. The Netherlands: Elsevier Science Publishers.

Rodrik, Dani. 1997. *Has Globalization Gone Too Far?* Washington: Institute for International Economics.

Rogowski, Ronald. 1987. Political Cleavages and Changing Exposure to Trade. *American Political Science Review* 81, no. 4 (December): 1121-37.

Rogowski, Ronald. 1989. *Commerce and Coalitions.* Princeton, NJ: Princeton University Press.

Rubin, Donald B. 1987. *Multiple Imputation for Nonresponse in Surveys.* New York: J. Wiley & Sons.

Rybczynski, T. M. 1955. Factor Endowments and Relative Commodity Prices. *Economica* 22: 336-41.

Sapiro, Virginia, Steven J. Rosenstone, Warren E. Miller, and the National Election Studies. 1998. American National Election Studies, 1948-1997 [CD-ROM], ed. ICPSR. Ann Arbor, MI: Inter-university Consortium for Political and Social Research [producer and distributor].

Scheve, Kenneth F. 2000. Comparative Context and Public Preferences over Regional Economic Integration. Paper presented at the 2000 annual meeting of the American Political Science Association, Washington (August).

Scheve, Kenneth F., and Matthew J. Slaughter. 2001a. What Determines Individual Trade-Policy Preferences. *Journal of International Economics,* forthcoming.

Scheve, Kenneth F., and Matthew J. Slaughter. 2001b. "Labor-Market Competition and Individual Preferences Over Immigration Policy. *Review of Economics and Statistics,* 83, no. 1 (February): 133-46.

Schafer, Joseph L. 1997. *Analysis of Incomplete Multivariate Data.* London: Chapman & Hall.

Scholl, Russell B. 2000. The International Investment Position of the United States at Year-end 1999. *Survey of Current Business* (July): 46-56.

Schuman, Howard, and Stanley Presser. 1981. *Questions and Answers in Attitude Surveys.* New York: Wiley.

Sekhon, Jasjeet. 1999. *The Economic Sophistication of American Politics: American Public Opinion and Monetary Policy, 1973-1993.* Ph.D. dissertation, Department of Government, Cornell University.

Skinner, Jonathan. 1994. Housing and Saving in the United States. In *Housing Markets in the United States and Japan*, ed. Yukio Noguchi and James M. Poterba. Chicago: University of Chicago Press.

Slaughter, Matthew J. 2000a. What Are the Results of Product-Price Studies and What Can We Learn from Their Differences? In *The Impact of International Trade on Wages*, NBER Conference Volume, ed. Robert C. Feenstra. Cambridge, MA: National Bureau of Economic Research.

Slaughter, Matthew J. 2000b. Production Transfer within Multinational Enterprises and American Wages. *Journal of International Economics* 50, no. 2 (April): 449-72.

Smith, Alasdair. 1984. Capital Theory and Trade Theory. In *Handbook of International Economics*, vol. 1, ed. Ronald W. Jones and Peter B. Kenen. Amsterdam: Elsevier Science Publishers.

Sniderman, Paul, Richard Brody, and Philip Tetlock. 1991. *Reasoning and Choice: Explorations in Political Psychology*. New York: Cambridge University Press.

Stolper, Wolfgang, and Paul Samuelson. 1941. Protection and Real Wages. *Review of Economic Studies* 9 (November): 58-73.

Sullivan, John, James Pierson, and George Marcus. 1978. Ideological Constraint in the Mass Public. *American Journal of Political Science* 22, no. 2: 233-49.

Timmer, Ashley, and Jeffrey Williamson. 1998. Immigration Policy Prior to the 1930s: Labor Markets, Policy Interactions, and Global Backlash. *Population and Development Review* 24, no. 4: 739-71.

Verdier, Daniel. 1994. *Democracy and International Trade: Britain, France, and the United States, 1860-1990*. Princeton, NJ: Princeton University Press.

Wallach, Lori, and Michelle Sforza. 1999. *Whose Trade Organization?: Corporate Globalization and the Erosion of Democracy*. Washington: Public Citizen, Inc.

Zaller, John. 1992. *The Nature and Origins of Mass Opinion*. Cambridge, England: Cambridge University Press.

Index

immigrants
  local concentration of, 71-72 (See also
    gateway communities)
  skill mix of, 72-74, 102
immigration
  gateway communities, 52-53, 55, 71-72,
    75, 104
  globalization in terms of, 2, 3f
  immigration shock, size of, 103-04
  impact on wages, 51-53, 85-86, 93, 103-
    04
  public knowledge about, 43
  public opinion about, 35-37, 44
  restrictions on, 6
Immigration Opinion, 56, 57t, 69
  noneconomic determinants of, 69, 109
immigration policy preferences
  analysis of, summary statistics for, 56,
    57t
  area-analysis model, 52-53, 71-72, 73t
  determinants of, 69, 70t
  factor-proportions-analysis model, 52,
    69, 70t
  and income, 51-53, 102-04
  multiple imputation methodology,
    114-15
  robustness checks for, 72-75, 109
  and skill level, 51-53, 55, 58, 69-71, 70t-
    71t
imports
  labor-market costs of, 18
  as share of GDP, 2, 2f
income
  immigration policy and, 51-53, 102-04
  labor, current, 48
  trade policy and, 48-51, 99-102
income distribution, effect of trade on, 92
income inequality. See skills premium;
    wages
industry. See also specific industry (e.g.
    steel, textiles)
  adjustment assistance for, 96
  factor incomes of, 48-49
  local mix, and housing prices, 105
  nontraded, jobs in, 15-16, 49, 50-51
  trade exposure, and policy preferences,
    55, 57-59, 62-63, 75
interest-group politics, 65
intersectoral factor mobility, 48-49, 102
IP (data augmentation method), 113

job creation, 17-20
  effect of foreign direct investment on,
    38-41
job destruction, 17-20, 23-24, 44

effect of foreign direct investment on,
    38-41
jobs
  implementation of trade barriers to
    protect, 23-26, 88-89
  kinds of, versus number of, 19, 41
  in nontraded industries, effect of trade
    on, 15-16
  reallocation of, 19, 41, 96

labor demand
  cross-industry shifts in, 49
  and relative wages, 49
labor force, skill mix of, 83, 83t
labor market attachment, and
    immigration policy, 74-75
labor-market pressures, 77-86. See also
    worker perceptions/pressures
  adjustment assistance for, 94-96
  created by foreign direct investment,
    37-41, 44
  created by immigration, 35-37, 44
  effect on policy perceptions, 87-92
  public acceptance of, to protect prices,
    23
  role of globalization in, 10-11
labor markets
  costs of trade for, public perception of,
    17-20, 44
  high-immigration, 58-59
  local
    definition of, 108
    and immigration policy, 52-53
labor market skills. See skill levels
labor mobility, 51, 63, 102
labor productivity, growth in, 10, 84-85
listwise deletion, 111
living standards, 90-91

macroeconomic performance,
    globalization backlash and, 77-78
manufacturing
  average wages, 100, 100f
  productivity slowdown in, 84-85
  skills premium in, 78, 79f
media, influence on public opinion, 93
mercantilist attitudes, 16, 16n, 35
metropolitan statistical area (MSA), 55
Missing at Random (MAR), 112n
Missing Completely at Random (MCAR),
    112n
Multifiber Arrangement, 5, 93
Multilateral Agreement on Investment, 6
multinational corporations, 94, 1-2, 37-41

multiple imputation, 111-15
  in immigration policy analysis, 114-15
  procedures for, 111-12, 112n
  in trade policy analysis, 112-14

NAFTA. *See* North American Free Trade
  Agreement (NAFTA)
National Bureau of Economic Research
  (NBER), 108
National Election Studies (NES) surveys,
  53-57, 117
  immigration policy, 54
  incomplete/missing data, analysis of,
  112-15
  policy preference questions, 54
New York Stock Exchange, 77
nontraded sectors, 99-100
  jobs in, 15-16
North American Free Trade Agreement
  (NAFTA), 6, 30-32

Occupation Wage, 55
  and immigration policy, 69, 70t, 71t,
  73t
  and trade policy, 56t, 57t, 59t, 60t, 60n,
  61t, 62t, 64t
Organization for Economic Cooperation
  and Development, 6
output mix, 102-04
outsourcing, 86

Party Identification
  definition of, 109
  and immigration policy, 70t, 72, 73t
  and trade policy, 63, 63n, 64t
permanent normal trade relations
  (PNTR) status, to China, 5, 29-30, 35
Perot, Ross, 6
policy actions
  distinction between policy preferences
  and, 8n-9n
  link between policy preferences and, 8,
  94
policy cleavages, 47-76
  further evidence of, 117-18
  theory of, 99-105
policy preferences, 13-45. *See also* public
  perception
  distinction between policy actions and,
  8n-9n
  effect of labor-market pressures on, 87-
  92
  effect of skill level on, 9-10, 59-63, 87
  policy implications, 94-96

  employment sector and, 50-51, 55, 99-
  100
  facts about, 14-27
  forward-thinking, 92-93
  and globalization backlash, 7-8
  immigration (*See* immigration policy
  preferences)
  influence of media/political leaders
  on, 93
  key features of, 44
  knowledge level and uncertainty
  factors, 41-44, 42n-43n, 44, 93n
  labor-market skills and, 9-10
  policy actions and, 8
  protectionism *versus* free traders, 28,
  44, 96
  theory of, 47-53
  trade (*See* trade policy preferences)
political awareness, 65-66
  measurement of, 66
political trade barriers, decline of, 3
political control variables, 63n, 63-66, 109
political ideology. *See Ideology*
political leaders, influence on public
  opinion, 93
political party identification. *See Party
  Identification*
polling. *See* public opinion surveys
price index, for nominal to real wages,
  80
prices
  changes in, and wage trends, 85, 99
  effect of trade policy on, 14-15, 23, 26
  factor, 103-04
  factor incomes and, 49
  housing (*See* housing prices)
  nontraded products, 99-100
  protection of, and labor-market
  pressures, 23
  world product, 103
production, factors of, 104
productivity, labor, growth in, 10
productivity measures, 84-85
product prices. *See* prices
product quality, 15
product variety, 14
Proposition 187 (California), 6
protectionist policy, efficacy of, public
  faith in, 29, 93
public knowledge, effect on public
  opinion, 41-43, 42n-43n, 44, 93n
public opinion. *See* policy preferences;
  public perception

Public Opinion Databank (Roper Center
for Public Opinion Research), 13, 107
public opinion surveys, 13, 87
  framing of questions for, 27-29
  historical data, 88-92
public perception, 13-45. *See also* policy
  preferences
  of costs *versus* benefits of trade, 20-26,
    44
  of foreign direct investment, 37-41, 44
  of immigration, 35-37, 44
  of labor-market costs of trade, 17-20,
    44
  of trade benefits, 14-16, 44
public protests
  at World Bank Washington meeting, 4-
    5, 7
  at WTO Seattle meeting, 4-5, 7, 94

Race
  definition of, 109
  and immigration policy, 70*t*, 73*t*
  and trade policy, 64*t*
racial tolerance, 75
real-wage growth, 10-11, 78-84
  technological change as cause of, 90-
    93
Ricardo-Viner (RV) framework, 48-51
  and policy cleavage, 50-51, 101-02,
    102*n*
robustness checks, 53-59, 109
  for immigration policy preferences, 72-
    75, 109
  for trade policy preferences, 63-66, 109
Roper Center for Public Opinion
  Research, Public Opinion Databank,
    13, 107

sector bias, 50-51, 55, 99-100, 101*n*
Sector Net Export Share, 55, 56*t*, 59*t*, 61*t*,
  62*t*, 64*t*
  construction of, 108
sectors
  nontraded, 99-100
  jobs in, 15-16
  services, 78
Sector Tariff, 55, 56*t*, 59*t*, 61*t*, 62*t*, 64*t*
  construction of, 108
skill groups, adjustment assistance for,
  94-96
skill levels, 49-50
  effect on policy preferences, 9-10, 59-
    63, 87
  policy implications, 94-96

of immigrants, 72-74, 102
and immigration policy preferences,
  51-53, 55, 58, 69-71, 70*t*-71*t*
labor force mix of, 83, 83*t*
measurement of, 49-50, 54-55, 59
real-wage performance across, 81-83,
  82*f*
tariff rates by, 100-01, 101*f*
and technological change, 10-11, 78, 84,
  85-86
and wage premium, 10-11, 78
wage trends across, 78-84
skills premium, 10-11, 78-84
  effect of globalization on, 85, 91
  in manufacturing, 78, 79*f*
Standard Industrial Classification (SIC),
  108
steel industry, 24
Stolper-Samuelson theorem, 43*n*, 85, 99,
  103

tariff rates, 55
  general issue of, public opinion about,
    89-90
  by industry skill level, 100-01, 101*f*
technological change
  as cause of slow wage growth, 90-93
  skill-biased, 10-11, 78, 84, 85-86
textiles, 5-6, 93, 101
time-series evidence, on public support
  for trade liberalization, 88-92
trade
  benefits of, public perception of, 14-16,
    44
  costs *versus* benefits, public perception
    of, 20-26
  international emphasis on, *versus* US
    focus, 33-35, 44
  labor-market costs of, public
    perception of, 17-20
  lack of knowledge about, 41-43, 42*n*-
    43*n*, 93*n*
Trade Act of 1974, 4
Trade Adjustment Assistance (TAA)
  program, 96
trade barriers
  decline of, 3
  implementation of
    and costs *versus* benefits of trade, 22-
      23, 44
    to protect jobs and wages, 23-26, 88-
      89
  for specific industries, 24-26

Other Publications from the Institute for International Economics

*= out of print

POLICY ANALYSES IN INTERNATIONAL ECONOMICS Series

Subsidies in International Trade*
Gary Clyde Hufbauer and Joanna Shelton Erb
1984   ISBN 0-88132-004-8
International Debt: Systemic Risk and Policy
Response*   William R. Cline
1984   ISBN 0-88132-015-3
Trade Protection in the United States: 31 Case
Studies*   Gary Clyde Hufbauer, Diane E.
Berliner, and Kimberly Ann Elliott
1986   ISBN 0-88132-040-4
Toward Renewed Economic Growth in Latin
America*   Bela Balassa, Gerardo M. Bueno, Pedro-
Pablo Kuczynski, and Mario Henrique Simonsen
1986   ISBN 0-88132-045-5
Capital Flight and Third World Debt*
Donald R. Lessard and John Williamson, editors
1987   ISBN 0-88132-053-6
The Canada-United States Free Trade Agreement:
The Global Impact*
Jeffrey J. Schott and Murray G. Smith, editors
1988   ISBN 0-88132-073-0
World Agricultural Trade: Building a Consensus*
William M. Miner and Dale E. Hathaway, editors
1988   ISBN 0-88132-071-3
Japan in the World Economy*
Bela Balassa and Marcus Noland
1988   ISBN 0-88132-041-2
America in the World Economy: A Strategy for
the 1990s*   C. Fred Bergsten
1988   ISBN 0-88132-089-7
Managing the Dollar: From the Plaza to the
Louvre*   Yoichi Funabashi
1988, 2d ed. 1989   ISBN 0-88132-097-8
United States External Adjustment and the World
Economy*   William R. Cline
May 1989   ISBN 0-88132-048-X
Free Trade Areas and U.S. Trade Policy*
Jeffrey J. Schott, editor
May 1989   ISBN 0-88132-094-3
Dollar Politics: Exchange Rate Policymaking in
the United States*
I.M. Destler and C. Randall Henning
September 1989   ISBN 0-88132-079-X
Latin American Adjustment: How Much Has
Happened?*   John Williamson, editor
April 1990   ISBN 0-88132-125-7
The Future of World Trade in Textiles and
Apparel*   William R. Cline
1987, 2d ed. June 1990   ISBN 0-88132-110-9
Completing the Uruguay Round: A Results-
Oriented Approach to the GATT Trade
Negotiations*   Jeffrey J. Schott, editor
September 1990   ISBN 0-88132-130-3

Economic Sanctions Reconsidered (2 volumes)
Economic Sanctions Reconsidered: Supplemental
Case Histories
Gary Clyde Hufbauer, Jeffrey J. Schott, and
Kimberly Ann Elliott
1985, 2d ed. Dec. 1990   ISBN cloth 0-88132-115-X
                           ISBN paper 0-88132-105-2
Economic Sanctions Reconsidered: History and
Current Policy
Gary Clyde Hufbauer, Jeffrey J. Schott, and
Kimberly Ann Elliott
December 1990   ISBN cloth 0-88132-140-0
                           ISBN paper 0-88132-136-2
Pacific Basin Developing Countries: Prospects for
the Future*   Marcus Noland
January 1991   ISBN cloth 0-88132-141-9
                           ISBN 0-88132-081-1
Currency Convertibility in Eastern Europe*
John Williamson, editor
October 1991   ISBN 0-88132-128-1
International Adjustment and Financing: The
Lessons of 1985-1991*   C. Fred Bergsten, editor
January 1992   ISBN 0-88132-112-5
North American Free Trade: Issues and
Recommendations*
Gary Clyde Hufbauer and Jeffrey J. Schott
April 1992   ISBN 0-88132-120-6
Narrowing the U.S. Current Account Deficit*
Allen J. Lenz
June 1992   ISBN 0-88132-103-6
The Economics of Global Warming
William R. Cline/June 1992   ISBN 0-88132-132-X
U.S. Taxation of International Income: Blueprint
for Reform*   Gary Clyde Hufbauer, assisted by
Joanna M. van Rooij
October 1992   ISBN 0-88132-134-6
Who's Bashing Whom? Trade Conflict in High-
Technology Industries   Laura D'Andrea Tyson
November 1992   ISBN 0-88132-106-0
Korea in the World Economy*   Il SaKong
January 1993   ISBN 0-88132-183-4
Pacific Dynamism and the International
Economic System*
C. Fred Bergsten and Marcus Noland, editors
May 1993   ISBN 0-88132-196-6
Economic Consequences of Soviet
Disintegration*
John Williamson, editor
May 1993   ISBN 0-88132-190-7
Reconcilable Differences? United States-Japan
Economic Conflict*
C. Fred Bergsten and Marcus Noland
June 1993   ISBN 0-88132-129-X
Does Foreign Exchange Intervention Work?
Kathryn M. Dominguez and Jeffrey A. Frankel
September 1993   ISBN 0-88132-104-4

Summitry in the Americas: A Progress Report
Richard E. Feinberg
April 1997   ISBN 0-88132-242-3
Corruption and the Global Economy
Kimberly Ann Elliott
June 1997   ISBN 0-88132-233-4
Regional Trading Blocs in the World Economic
System   Jeffrey A. Frankel
October 1997   ISBN 0-88132-202-4
Sustaining the Asia Pacific Miracle:
Environmental Protection and Economic
Integration   André Dua and Daniel C. Esty
October 1997   ISBN 0-88132-250-4
Trade and Income Distribution   William R. Cline
November 1997   ISBN 0-88132-216-4
Global Competition Policy
Edward M. Graham and J. David Richardson
December 1997   ISBN 0-88132-166-4
Unfinished Business: Telecommunications after
the Uruguay Round
Gary Clyde Hufbauer and Erika Wada
December 1997   ISBN 0-88132-257-1
Financial Services Liberalization in the WTO
Wendy Dobson and Pierre Jacquet
June 1998   ISBN 0-88132-254-7
Restoring Japan's Economic Growth
Adam S. Posen
September 1998   ISBN 0-88132-262-8
Measuring the Costs of Protection in China
Zhang Shuguang, Zhang Yansheng, and Wan
Zhongxin
November 1998   ISBN 0-88132-247-4
Foreign Direct Investment and Development: The
New Policy Agenda for Developing Countries
and Economies in Transition
Theodore H. Moran
December 1998   ISBN 0-88132-258-X
Behind the Open Door: Foreign Enterprises in the
Chinese Marketplace   Daniel H. Rosen
January 1999   ISBN 0-88132-263-6
Toward A New International Financial
Architecture: A Practical Post-Asia Agenda
Barry Eichengreen
February 1999   ISBN 0-88132-270-9
Is the U.S. Trade Deficit Sustainable?
Catherine L. Mann/*September 1999*
ISBN 0-88132-265-2
Safeguarding Prosperity in a Global Financial
System: The Future International Financial
Architecture, Independent Task Force Report
Sponsored by the Council on Foreign Relations
Morris Goldstein, Project Director
October 1999   ISBN 0-88132-287-3
Avoiding the Apocalypse: The Future of the Two
Koreas   Marcus Noland
June 2000   ISBN 0-88132-278-4

Assessing Financial Vulnerability: An Early
Warning System for Emerging Markets
Morris Goldstein, Graciela Kaminsky, and Carmen
Reinhart
June 2000   ISBN 0-88132-237-7
Global Electronic Commerce: A Policy Primer
Catherine L. Mann, Sue E. Eckert, and Sarah
Cleeland Knight
July 2000   ISBN 0-88132-274-1
The WTO after Seattle
Jeffrey J. Schott, editor
July 2000   ISBN 0-88132-290-3
Intellectual Property Rights in the Global
Economy   Keith E. Maskus
August 2000   ISBN 0-88132-282-2
The Political Economy of the Asian Financial
Crisis   Stephan Haggard
August 2000   ISBN 0-88132-283-0
Transforming Foreign Aid: United States
Assistance in the 21st Century   Carol Lancaster
August 2000   ISBN 0-88132-291-1
Fighting the Wrong Enemy: Antiglobal Activists
and Multinational Enterprises
Edward M. Graham
September 2000   ISBN 0-88132-272-5
Globalization and the Perceptions of American
Workers
Kenneth F. Scheve and Matthew J. Slaughter
March 2001   ISBN-0-88132-295-4

SPECIAL REPORTS

1   Promoting World Recovery: A Statement on
     Global Economic Strategy*
     by Twenty-six Economists from Fourteen
     Countries
     December 1982   ISBN 0-88132-013-7
2   Prospects for Adjustment in Argentina,
     Brazil, and Mexico: Responding to the Debt
     Crisis*   John Williamson, editor
     June 1983   ISBN 0-88132-016-1
3   Inflation and Indexation: Argentina, Brazil,
     and Israel*   John Williamson, editor
     March 1985   ISBN 0-88132-037-4
4   Global Economic Imbalances*
     C. Fred Bergsten, editor
     March 1986   ISBN 0-88132-042-0
5   African Debt and Financing*
     Carol Lancaster and John Williamson, editors
     May 1986   ISBN 0-88132-044-7
6   Resolving the Global Economic Crisis: After
     Wall Street*
     Thirty-three Economists from Thirteen
     Countries
     December 1987   ISBN 0-88132-070-6

**Australia, New Zealand, and
Papua New Guinea**
D.A. INFORMATION SERVICES
648 Whitehorse Road
Mitcham, Victoria 3132, Australia
tel: 61-3-9210-7777
fax: 61-3-9210-7788
e-mail: service@dadirect.com.au
http://www.dadirect.com.au

Argentina
World Publications SA.
Av. Cordoba 1877
1120 Buenos Aires, Argentina
tel/fax: (54 11) 4815 8156
e-mail:
http://wpbooks@infovia.com.ar

Canada
RENOUF BOOKSTORE
5369 Canotek Road, Unit 1,
Ottawa, Ontario K1J 9J3, Canada
tel: 613-745-2665
fax: 613-745-7660
http://www.renoufbooks.com

Caribbean
SYSTEMATICS STUDIES LIMITED
St. Augustine Shopping Centre
Eastern Main Road, St. Augustine
Trinidad and Tobago, West Indies
tel: 868-645-8466
fax: 868-645-8467
e-mail: tobe@trinidad.net

People's Republic of China
(including Hong
Kong) **and Taiwan** (sales
representatives):
Tom Cassidy
Cassidy & Associates
70 Battery Place, Ste 220
New York, NY 10280
tel: 212-706-2200   fax: 212-706-2254
e-mail: CHINACAS@Prodigy.net

Colombia, Ecuador, and Peru
Infoenlace Ltda
Attn: Octavio Rojas
Calle 72 No. 13-23 Piso 3
Edificio Nueva Granada, Bogota, D.C.
Colombia
tel: (571) 255 8783 or 255 7969
fax: (571) 248 0808 or 217 6435

**United Kingdom and Europe
(including Russia and Turkey)**
The Eurospan Group
3 Henrietta Street, Covent Garden
London WC2E 8LU England
tel: 44-20-7240-0856
fax: 44-20-7379-0609
http://www.eurospan.co.uk

**India, Bangladesh, Nepal, and Sri
Lanka**
Viva Books Pvt.
Mr. Vinod Vasishtha
4325/3, Ansari Rd.
Daryaganj, New Delhi-110002
INDIA
tel: 91-11-327-9280
fax: 91-11-326-7224 ,
e-mail: vinod.viva@gndel.globalnet.
ems.vsnl.net.in

Japan and the Republic of Korea
United Publishers Services, Ltd.
Kenkyu-Sha Bldg.
9, Kanda Surugadai 2-Chome
Chiyoda-Ku, Tokyo 101
JAPAN
tel: 81-3-3291-4541;
fax: 81-3-3292-8610
e-mail: saito@ups.co.jp
**For trade accounts only.
Individuals will find IIE books in
leading Tokyo bookstores.**

**Northern Africa and the Middle
East** (Egypt, Algeria, Bahrain,
Palestine, Jordan, Kuwait, Lebanon,
Libya, Morocco, Oman, Qatar,
Saudi Arabia, Syria, Tunisia,
Yemen, and United Arab Emirates)
Middle East Readers Information
Center (MERIC)
2 bahgat Aly Street
El-Masry Towers, Tower #D, Apt.
#24, First Floor
Zamalek, Cairo EGYPT
tel: 202-341-3824/340 3818;
fax 202-341-9355
http://www.meric-co.com

South Africa
Pat Bennink
Dryad Books
PO Box 11684
Vorna Valley 1686
South Africa
tel: +27 14 576 1332
fax: +27 82 899 9156
e-mail: dryad@hixnet.co.za

South America
Julio E. Emod
Publishers Marketing & Research
Associates, c/o HARBRA
Rua Joaquim Tavora, 629
04015-001 Sao Paulo, Brasil
tel: (55) 11-571-1122;
fax: (55) 11-575-6876
e-mail: emod@harbra.com.br

Taiwan
Unifacmanu Trading Co., Ltd.
4F, No. 91, Ho-Ping East Rd, Sect. 1
Taipei 10609, Taiwan
tel: 886-2-23419646
fax: 886-2-23943103
e-mail: winjoin@ms12.hinet.net

Thailand
Asia Books 5 Sukhumvit Rd. Soi 61
Bangkok 10110 Thailand
(phone 662-714-0740-2 Ext: 221, 222,
223
fax: (662) 391-2277)
e-mail: purchase@asiabooks.co.th
http://www.asiabooksonline.com

**Visit our Web site at:
http://www.iie.com
E-mail orders to:
orders@iie.com**